PLANNING MICRONESIA'S FUTURE

PLANNING MICRONESIA'S FUTURE

A Summary of the United States Commercial Company's
Economic Survey of Micronesia, 1946

Douglas L. Oliver, Editor

Edwin H. Bryan, Edward E. Gallahue, Howard G. MacMillan
Leonard E. Mason, Karl J. Pelzer, Robert O. Smith, John Useem
Mrs. Ella Embree and Miss Velma Ryan, Editorial Assistants

Harvard University Press
Cambridge, Massachusetts
1951

Manufactured in the United States of America

INTRODUCTION

Shortly after V-J Day the United States Naval Command in the Pacific requested the United States Commercial Company (USCC) to undertake an economic survey of Guam and the former Japanese Mandated Islands in order to assist Naval Military Government in its task of administering these islands. The USCC, a branch of the wartime Foreign Economic Administration, had been active in the Pacific Islands since 1942, assisting in the development of local economic resources and in the support of island civilian economies, so that there were staff and other facilities already available in the field for carrying out some of this Survey. In addition, specialists from other Federal organizations and from nongovernmental institutions were borrowed in order to cover expertly the very wide range of subjects required for a comprehensive survey. Listed below are the specialists who participated in the Survey and the institutions with which they were associated:

Dr. Elmer Alpert, nutritionist, United States Public Health Service
Dr. William R. Bascom, anthropologist, Northwestern University
Dr. Josiah Bridge, geologist, Department of the Interior
Mr. Edwin H. Bryan, geographer, USCC
Dr. F. R. Fosberg, botanist, USCC
Commander E. E. Gallahue, economist, on leave from Department of Agriculture
Mr. P. A. Gantt, animal husbandry specialist, USCC, on leave from University of Hawaii
Dr. E. T. Hall, Jr., anthropologist, University of Denver
Mr. E. Y. Hosaka, botanist, University of Hawaii
Mr. Richard Lyman, agronomist, USCC
Dr. H. G. MacMillan, agriculturist, USCC
Mr. W. D. Mark, mining engineer, Reconstruction Finance Corporation
Mr. L. E. Mason, anthropologist, Department of State
Mr. R. G. Oakley, entomologist, Department of Agriculture
Dr. Douglas L. Oliver, special representative, Pacific Ocean areas, USCC
Dr. K. J. Pelzer, geographer, Department of Agriculture
Dr. A. M. Piper, water resources geologist, Department of the Interior
Mr. J. C. Ripperton, agronomist, Hawaiian Agricultural Experiment Station
Mr. O. C. Rogers, soils scientist, Department of Agriculture
Mr. R. O. Smith, fisheries specialist, Department of the Interior
Dr. H. K. Townes, entomologist, Department of Agriculture
Mr. Howard Trueblood, economist, USCC
Dr. John Useem, sociologist, University of Wisconsin

Technical assistance in the field was furnished by Mr. Paul Breese, Mr. Kaoru Uyehara, Mr. Clarence Wong, Mr. Anthony Aki, Mr. Simon Provincher, and by members of the field staff of the USCC stationed throughout the islands.

Under the leadership of Mr. Richard B. Black, some of the specialists visited the principal islands in an LCI loaned by the Navy. Others, including all the social scientists, traveled separately according to their needs or remained in one location for the duration of the Survey. It was recognized that an appraisal of natural resources, such as that carried out in survey fashion by the natural scientists, would be meaningless without some consideration of the manner in which such resources were to be utilized by the native residents. It was also clearly recognized that Micronesia was lacking in any uniform pattern regarding the economic needs and institutions of its inhabitants and that much weight must be given to this circumstance when planning the utilization of resources. It was accordingly decided that each social scientist would remain in one area long enough to make the more intensive kind of investigations required for providing the sociological background against which the findings of the other specialists could be projected.

The Survey lasted throughout the spring and summer of 1946. Upon its completion, each expert wrote a report on his own subject, after which an editorial board, selected from Survey members (Messrs. Edwin H. Bryan, Edward E. Gallahue, Howard G. MacMillan, Leonard E. Mason, Douglas L. Oliver, Karl J. Pelzer, Robert O. Smith, and John Useem), distilled from the thousands of pages[1] the following summary. Each board member prepared one or more sections, incorporating board recommendations along with data from all reports, and each section was then edited and revised at board meetings. Despite varying literary styles, the contents of all sections represent the consensus. Some of the sections overlap and irritating duplications occur, but the repetitions were not all eliminated because in some instances emphasis is desirable – particularly because of the interdependence of subject matters – and, in others, elimination would have done violence to the author's presentation.

Final answers are not to be found in this summary of a survey which was of necessity merely exploratory. Some recommendations are definitive enough, but most sections only formulate the problems and propose methods for seeking solutions. The present tense is frequently used throughout the text, and it should be understood that it refers to the time when field investigation took place (May - August 1946). Between that time and the date when this book went to press a number of changes took place in American Micronesia. Some of the more important of these changes have been given in notes at the ends of the chapters. Others have been described in "The Handbook on the Trust Territory of the Pacific Islands"[2] and in the Annual Reports to the United Nations on the administration of the Trust Territory of the Pacific Islands and of Guam, prepared by the Navy Department.

As it stands, this Summary is certainly no prose masterpiece. (Its purposes were practical, not literary.) It is nevertheless a notable document on several counts, and the Harvard University Press deserves more than passing credit in undertaking its publication at this late date.

For one thing, the Survey represents the successful pooling of the knowledge and observations of many different kinds of specialists all working on one highly complex problem. Its subject matter is the lives and welfare of thousands of innocent victims of an international rivalry beyond their understanding and even further beyond their control. Its objective is the sobering one of attempting to prescribe a way of life for people who have no effective voice in deciding their own destinies.

Another noteworthy though incidental fact about this document has been its effect: now, four years after it was written, there is evidence that many of its recommendations are actually being carried out – a rare and exhilarating experience for most scientists who venture into the practical world of affairs.

Special acknowledgments are due the following persons who assisted materially in carrying out the Survey:

From United States Commercial Company: Mrs. Ella Embree, Miss Velma Ryan, Mr. G. R. Parker, Mr. H. E. Bishop, and Mr. Arthur Z. Gardiner.

1. Typescript; microfilm copies of all subject reports are on file in the Library of Congress, Washington, D.C.

2. Published by the Navy Department, 1948. The Navy Department continues in administrative control of the islands of the Trust Territory. On August 1, 1950, the Department of the Interior took over the reins of government on Guam.

From the United States Navy: Captain W. F. Jennings, Captain J. C. Hammock, Captain C. L. Winecoff, Rear Admiral John Whelchel, and the officers and crew of the LCI 983.

From the Bernice P. Bishop Museum, Honolulu: Dr. Peter Buck and Dr. K. P. Emory.

From the University of Hawaii: Mr. Howry Warner and Dr. James Shoemaker.

Cambridge, Massachusetts
February 1950

Douglas L. Oliver
Director of Survey

CONTENTS

CHAPTER I. GEOGRAPHIC AND HUMAN SETTINGS

A. GEOGRAPHIC SUMMARY

The Marshall, Caroline, and Mariana Islands are located north of the equator and west of the 180th meridian, in the North Pacific Ocean. They lie scattered over an oceanic area larger than the United States, but altogether comprise a land area of only 901.4 square miles. All areas and distances in this geographic summary are in statute miles.

The islands fall into three main categories: atolls, single low islands, and high volcanic islands.

Group	No. of atolls	Single low islands	High volcanic islands	Complex assem-blages	Total no. of islets	Total land area in square miles
Marshalls	29	5	-	-	1156	70
Carolines	30	12	1	4	952	461.4
Marianas	-	-	15	-	29	370
	59	17	16	4	2137	901.4

In addition to dry land area there are nearly 7800 square miles of protected water of shallow or moderate depth, occurring mostly as lagoons delimitated by atolls or barrier reefs.

The Marshall Islands are easternmost of the three groups. They consist of two nearly parallel chains of islands, extending irregularly from north to south, an eastern or Ratak ("sunrise") chain and a western or Ralik ("sunset") chain. The twenty-nine atolls and five single low islands contain only seventy square miles of dry land area, yet cover a sea area extending over 180,000 square miles. This is truly "islandia."

The Caroline Islands stretch in a narrow band for a distance of 2200 miles from east to west, just north of the equator. The group consists of thirty atolls, twelve single low coral islands (one of these, Fais, is raised reef), one single "high" volcanic island (Kusaie), and four complex assemblages of islands (Ponape, Truk, Yap, and Palau). Ponape and Yap are intermediate in physiography between Kusaie and Truk. Whereas all the small islets of Kusaie are connected by platform reef with the main mass (Ualan), Ponape has several detached small islands lying within the barrier reef; and Yap is broken into four main islands and a dozen islets, all separated by very narrow channels and surrounded by a broad, fringing platform reef, into which there are a half dozen deep channels.

Truk is probably the most interesting island complex in Micronesia, if not in the world. It is not an atoll, but a group of high volcanic and low coral and sand islands and reefs surrounded by a barrier reef, on which there are nearly fifty low coral and sand islets. The barrier reef bears a close resemblance to an atoll, but the presence of the high islands within the lagoon rules out the use of the term "atoll." There are several entrances through the reef into the lagoon, much of which is of moderate depth, forming a spacious anchorage for large ships.

Palau, the largest assemblage in the Carolines, stretches some 104 miles from the northern side of Velasco Reef to the southwest corner of Angaur Island. It is narrow, with a greatest width of about eighteen miles. In the center of the group is the large island of Babelthuap, made up of rolling volcanic hills up to 700 feet elevation, with a land area of about 153 square miles. Toward the north end of the group is a small atoll (Kayangel Islands). The southern islands of the group are composed of raised reef (limestone). The line of transition between volcanic and limestone runs through the middle of Koror Island. Malakal, to the southwest of Koror, is an outlying bit of volcanic soil, and the southeastern corner of Babelthuap and adjacent small islands are composed of raised reef. The central southern islands are high and rugged; Angaur, much of Peleliu, and several near-by small islands are lower and less rugged.

The Mariana Islands comprise the southern third of the summits of a narrow range of volcanic mountains which extends southward from the southeastern corner of Honshu Island, Japan. The chain forms a slight crescent for a distance of about 600 miles from Uracas Island (Farallon de Pajaros) to Santa Rosa Reef, just south-southwest of Guam. The water is more than 12,000 feet deep to the west of the chain, and drops to even greater depths to the east. Nero Deep, to the southeast of Guam, has a depth of 32,177 feet. Since it runs in practically a straight line and is composed of narrow islands, the Marianas archipelago occupies a sea area of only a few thousand square miles.

Four general types of geologic structures are known in Micronesia: (1) low sand and reef islands, both single and as parts of atolls; (2) raised-reef islands; (3) islands of volcanic origin; and (4) Yap, which contains what appear to be older rocks, at least in part sedimentary. Some islands exhibit combinations of these materials, such as the southern Mariana Islands which are partly volcanic and partly raised-reef rock.

The mineral resources of the islands are correlated closely with their geologic structure. The only mineral products of the low coral islands (both single and parts of atolls) are coral sand and reef rock, used as building materials, principally in making roads and airfields. A few low islands have meager deposits of guano and phosphate. On some of the raised-reef islands there are more extensive phosphate deposits, such as those on Angaur, Peleliu, and Fais. (Fais is a small raised-reef island, about 60 to 65 feet at greatest elevation.) The volcanic islands of recent geologic age, some of which still have active craters, have few useful minerals besides small deposits of sulphur and, of course, building material in the form of lava rock and ash. Some of the older islands have deposits of such minerals as bauxite, manganese, iron, and other elements.

The eastern half of Micronesia lies in the southwestern part of the northeast trade-wind belt. The western half lies on the eastern fringe of the monsoon region. The climate in both regions is controlled by the seasonal movement of the sun north and south over the area in summer, causing a shift in the position of the doldrums and of the equatorial front.

Temperature, relative humidity, and barometric pressure are relatively uniform, with little significant range throughout the area. Storms occur more violently in the western part of Micronesia than in the eastern. Tropical hurricanes are said to "breed" in the west-central Carolines and to move in a northwesterly direction, with considerable violence, between the Marianas and the Philippines, in the direction of Japan and the Loo Choo Islands. They are most common in late summer and early fall, and cause considerable damage in the southern Mariana Islands and the western Carolines.

There are certain well-marked wet and dry zones. Wake Island lies in a dry area. The climate becomes progressively wetter as one goes southward. Part way south Ujelang and Guam have moderate rainfall. Ponape and Palau have heavy rainfall, as have Ebon and Kusaie. The rainfall in the atolls of the southern Marshalls and eastern Carolines is not as great as on the high islands of Kusaie and Ponape, because much of the rainfall of the latter is caused by the interception of moisture-laden winds by the high mountains. The mean annual rainfall at Truk is markedly less than that at Ponape and Palau, and in some years less even than that at Yap and Guam. The explanation for this may be that Truk is in a transition zone between the trade winds to the east and the monsoons to the west and does not experience the full rainfall influence of either.

The seasonal distribution of rainfall also varies with position. At Ocean Island, just south of the Trust Territory, there are two rainfall maxima, the larger in early winter and the smaller in midsummer. Jaluit and Ponape have a rather uniform rainfall throughout the seasons, with months of heavy rainfall alternating with months of lighter rainfall. Further west, Ujelang marks the beginning of a definite summer rainfall maximum, and this phenomenon becomes progressively more pronounced to the west, although Palau also has a winter maximum because of its closer proximity to the equator. In Guam nearly 60 per cent of the rain falls during the four months between July 1 and October 31.

The variation in seasonal wind direction is also significant for native economy. In winter the winds throughout the area are predominantly from the quadrant north to east. This is because the normal trade winds of this portion of the Pacific are reinforced by the northeast monsoons. During the summer the northeast monsoon is replaced by the southwest monsoon, which accounts for the reversal in wind direction in the western portion of the area. As one goes east, however, there is less and less monsoon effect and, except near the equator where the southeast trade winds may creep northward, the northeast trades continue to predominate.

The nature of the flora in Micronesia is dependent largely upon (1) the nature of the environment, (2) the proximity or remoteness from the continental centers of plant dispersal whence spread the ancestors of the plants, and (3) the degree of isolation of the island. The first factor accounts largely for the nature of the vegetation, the other two for its systematic relationship. Both factors have been counteracted on some islands and in some regions of other islands through the activities of man.

Botanists recognize several plant associations in Micronesia. From shore to mountain top of different types of islands they include:

1. Mangrove swamps around protected shores, principally of high islands protected by reefs.
2. Strand flora, practically the only type on low sand and coral islands and dominating the beaches of high islands.
3. Low, dense, scrubby forest of raised-reef islands.
4. Plants of the plains and valleys of high volcanic islands.
5. Savannah or open grassland of volcanic forehills and plateaus.
6. Montane forest of moist mountain slopes.
7. Rain forest on the upper slopes of high volcanic islands.
8. Summit bogs and dwarf cloud flora.

These types are so constant that they identify the environment. For example, on Guam and other islands having a mixture of volcanic and raised-reef geological formation, the origin of the soil can be recognized at once from the nature of the vegetation growing upon it. Each plant association is conditioned or limited by its environment.

The Indo-Malayan region is the center of dispersal for the bulk of the species of plants occurring naturally on Pacific Islands, including the relatives of those classes as endemic (not found elsewhere). Whether they traveled eastward (against winds and currents), floating on the water or through the air, or whether they migrated along "land bridges" which now have sunk beneath the waves leaving behind only the tops of former peaks, is a problem for the biogeographer. The closer one approaches to the distribution center, the greater becomes the number of closely related species. This, of course, applies only to high islands having an environment capable of maintaining such species. It is true, however, that the strand flora, which dominates the low islands, is made up largely of species also found on the shores of Indo-Malayan islands.

Much of the lowland flora has found its way to Pacific Islands recently through the agency of man. This not only includes the cultivated species, purposely introduced, but also the weeds which have arrived with shipping. For example, nearly 60 per cent of the flowering plants and ferns found on Guam were introduced by man. About half of them came from tropical America and about half from the Indo-Malayan region. The American elements arrived via the Spanish galleons which touched at Guam en route from Acapulco, Mexico, to Manila. Some plants found their way into surrounding islands of Micronesia from Guam, while others were imported directly by early western voyagers. This accounts for the presence on many islands of Micronesia of such cultivated plants of American origin as sweet potatoes, corn, tobacco, cacao, cassava, tomatoes, pineapple, arrowroot, custard apple, peanuts, papayas, and peppers, for numerous ornamental species, and for the many species of tropicopolitan weeds. Many similar species of oriental origin arrived from Manila. And, during the past quarter century, many plants have been introduced from Japan.

Before the coming of men to Micronesia the islands were but sparsely stocked with insects, birds, and mammals (only rats and bats); possibly all of these derived ultimately from the Indo-Malayan region. Natives brought with them their pigs, dogs, and fowl. Much later, westerners introduced cattle, oxen, a few horses, and superior strains of pigs – along with several insect pests which continue to make heavy inroads on native crops.

Marine animals are found in greater abundance and variety than the land fauna. Tuna and bonito school far offshore, while in protected waters live shellfish, bêche-de-mer, and fish of many kinds, all requiring careful conservation if they are to continue as a source of native food and income.

Such is the natural environment of Micronesia: limited in land area and in most of its resources.

B. POPULATION[1]

The total native population of Micronesia (73,132 as of summer 1946[2]) was once much larger than it is today. The best estimates indicate that, during the last century, the loss of population ranged from 50 per cent in the Marshalls to 75 per cent in the Carolines. Many of the now uninhabited islands formerly contained sizable populations and most of the occupied islands still have fewer natives than they had in ancient times.

The degree and speed of recovery in numbers vary considerably from group to group. During recent decades the native population of the Mandated Islands has increased moderately and Guam has grown rapidly. The birth rate for Micronesia as a whole exceeds the death rate. Nevertheless, none of the groups is larger at present than in the period prior to the coming of foreign control. The Mariana Islands have had the greatest proportional increase; the Marshalls, Palau Islands, and Ponape have made slight gains; but Yap, Truk, and many of the smaller groups have not been able to hold their own. These differentials between islands are due more to varying birth rates than to varying death rates. The contrasts in replacement rates are revealed partially by a comparison of the ratio of children to the entire population. Children under fifteen make up nearly 45 per cent of the Chamorros[3] on Guam and Saipan, and 43 per cent on Rota. Native children comprise 37 per cent on Palau, 34 per cent in the Marshalls, 31 per cent on Ponape, 30 per cent on Truk, and 22 per cent on Yap. The percentage of children is even lower on many of the isolated atolls scattered throughout the area. In the western Carolines, for example, Ulithi has less than 20 per cent and Sonsorol fewer than 10 per cent under the age of fifteen. On some islands there is a high incidence of infertility. More than half of the married women in the reproductive ages of life on Yap, and one out of five on Palau, are without children. This condition is not due to voluntary restriction of births. The natives greatly desire children and the infertile are deeply concerned over the inability to reproduce. Native leaders on islands undergoing major declines, such as Yap and Sonsorol, are worried over their future.

Mortality rates, though lower in recent decades than in the earlier years, are still quite high in the former Japanese Mandated Islands. Saipan and Rota have had higher death rates than Guam. On Yap and Truk, death rates exceed birth rates. Infant mortality has been especially high throughout the Mandated Islands. The Japanese reported that deaths among children under the age of two were, on the average, one-fourth of the births. The family census made by the survey on Palau disclosed that every other family has lost one child. High infant mortality rates were found on Rota, the Marshalls, Ponape, Truk, and Yap. Life expectancy is lower among women than among men in some sections of Micronesia. In part this is due to maternal mortality rates and, in part, to the very heavy work burdens customarily assigned to women.

The recent gains made throughout Micronesia in curtailing death rates were lost during the war. Though the number of war-inflicted casualties was not great, losses were felt on every island in the orbit of combat. Direct combat deaths were fewer than those brought about by the collapse of ordinary sanitary controls, medical care, and food supply. Mortality was particularly high among the very young and the very old. As yet there has been no major recovery from the recent setbacks. American emergency medical aid did insure the survival of large numbers who otherwise might have perished, but the American health program is not sufficient yet to assure a healthy, expanding population. It is less adequate than that of the prewar period on many of the islands. If the type of medical services and sanitary measures given on Guam could be extended to the other islands, native populations would benefit greatly. At present, medical services are least available where they are needed most. It is urged that special attention be directed toward reducing infant mortality. Decrease in the death rate can be accomplished more readily than increase in the birth rate. Japanese attempts to alter the birth rate were unsuccessful. Despite their failure, the matter should not be neglected entirely. It is urged that a special medical staff be designated to examine the causes of infertility, appraise the reasons for the breakdown of the Japanese program, and, if possible, devise means for overcoming the present situation.

There is no danger in the immediate period ahead of overpopulation in Micronesia. Should a sharp increase in native population occur in the next few generations, there would be, with better utilization, enough land to absorb the additions without any serious problem. The low islands tend to be more densely populated than the high islands, but if proper steps are made to preserve the resources for native subsistence and to make available the necessary technological equipment, the low islands can maintain numbers considerably in excess of their present population. The gain from larger populations would mean not only additional productive manpower, but also an expanding economy and a heightening in native morale.[4]

Dislocation of populations from their home communities occurred throughout Micronesia during the war. Few villages have been restored to their prewar condition. Permanent settlement of the native populations is one of the basic and first prerequisites for the restoration of the economy. It should be done at the earliest possible time. The traditional ecological pattern of Micronesia is one of many small villages rather than concentrated populations in a few large towns. Where towns did exist, such as on Guam and Koror, they were made up mainly of workers who held government jobs or were engaged in servicing the foreign group. It is to the interest of the natives to remain close to their land and home villages. The primary advantages of town life are that it makes more accessible to government a large labor supply and widens the range of cultural opportunities open to the natives. Both ends could be accomplished without building small cities of the Agaña (Guam) type. It is urged that the Administration refrain from the ever-present temptation to draw natives from their local villages into towns located at the seat of government. Moreover, it is recommended that, outside of Agaña, no other large native towns be developed in Micronesia.

Emphasis should be on the encouragement and assistance of natives in their efforts to restore their prewar villages. The relocation of such settlements should be based on the needs and wishes of the native population rather than on the interests of the Administration in improving access to native communities for administrative purposes. Within the areas designated as open for settlement, natives should be given complete freedom to decide the patterns of their villages. Experience has demonstrated to the natives what modes of residence are most satisfactory to them, taking into account the climate, the relations to the sources of subsistence, and their way of life. American conceptions of what constitutes an aesthetic arrangement should not override native requirements. The temporary camps built during the war could not take into account native desires; they were designed as emergency shelter when space was at a premium, the loyalty of the natives in doubt, and resources for construction at a minimum. They should not be used as the model of what natives want, were accustomed to before the war, or need for permanent living. They are substandard compared with village life in the past, artificially separate natives from their sources of livelihood, and restrict the normal functioning of native society. American help in establishing permanent settlements can take the following specific forms: the early determination of the lands free for village sites, assurance to natives through formal proceedings of the permanency of the locations approved, the releasing of natives from their present camps, the freeing of workers from other duties so that they can reconstruct their villages, the provision of essential equipment and materials, the establishment of Administration-sponsored services in the villages, and the reorganization of administrative programs to deal with a decentralized population.

The existing directive permitting complete freedom of movement[5] within the Micronesian islands is endorsed. No pressure should be exerted, however, to relocate natives away from their home islands and no involuntary evacuations should be tolerated. Natives should be informed of the opportunities open to them elsewhere; but they should be allowed to decide whether or not they wish to leave their traditional home islands for residence elsewhere. The practice of banishing natives from their home islands as a means of punishment has occurred and should be forbidden.

It is recommended that the directive on freedom of movement within Micronesia be expanded to include freedom to move outside of Micronesia. Natives wishing to visit the United States and its territorial possessions should be expected to pay their own expenses except where the trip is part of an Administration-sponsored educational program. Natives should be helped to the extent that they can obtain the necessary passports without undue delay. Guamians now find the delay in getting passports excessively prolonged. It is suggested that the State Department be invited to formulate a more effective procedure for getting passports than now exists.

Castoff dungarees, a smattering of English, and a mission handshake are not to be regarded as evidence of thorough Americanization; it must be remembered that Micronesians – all of them – are unlike Americans in many fundamental characteristics, and they cannot be expected to think or react like Americans at this stage of our contact with them. Agents of the Administration planning their economy and working with them must bear this in mind. Just as important is the consideration that Micronesian "culture" (that is, social organization, technology, language, values, material possessions, and so forth) may differ from island to island and hence that a tool or an industry or a regulation devised for one island may not be applicable to another.

There follows here a list of the several Culture Areas into which native communities may be grouped for the purpose of planning and applying programs of economic rehabilitation. The assumption is that all communities in a Culture Area have approximately similar needs, technologies, value systems, and so forth, and are in fact closely interrelated through economic, social, and political ties. In the list (Table I) that follows there have been grouped together into Administrative Units all Culture Areas which have similar – but not necessarily identical – cultures, or which were previously interrelated through economic ties.

TABLE I. POPULATION OF MICRONESIA, 1935[a] AND 1946,[b] BY CULTURE AREAS

	1935			1946[c]
	Japanese	Foreigners	Natives	Natives[d]
1. Marshalls Administrative Unit:				
Ralik Area	30	2	4,806	4,563
Radik Area	480	6	5,815	4,962
2. East Carolines Administrative Unit:				
Ponape Area (including Ant and Pakin Islands)	2,479	22	5,641	5,662
Ngatik Area	-	-	295	222
Mokil Area	-	-	258	428
Pingelap Area	4	-	694	1,651
Kusaie Area	25	6	1,189	1,555
Nukuoro Area	-	-	198	235
Kapingamarangi Area	1	-	399	441
Oroluk	38	-	4	-
3. Central Carolines Administrative Unit:				
Truk Island Area	1,978	14	10,344	9,750
Namoi Area	7	10	2,200	1,900
Namoluk Area	1	-	294	238
Losap Area	-	-	570	648
Nama Area	-	-	406	490
Hall Islands Area	-	-	445	477
Namonuito Area	1	-	303	246
Pulap Area	-	-	257	263
Puluwat Area	-	-	335	209
Pulusuk Area	-	-	194	211
4. Yap Administrative Unit:				
Yap Island Area	392	11	3,713	3,030
Ngulu Area	-	-	53	61
Ulithi Area	1	-	433	418
Fais Area	-	-	334	236
Sorol Area	-	-	8	12
Woleai Area	1	-	570	392
Eauripik Area	-	-	110	98
Ifalik Area	-	-	388	282
Faraulap Area	1	-	291	-
Elato Area	-	-	71	34
Lamotrek Area	1	-	192	152
Satawal Area	3	-	287	36
5. Palau Administrative Unit:				
Palau Area (including Babelthuap, Koror, Peleliu, Kayangel)	7,419	18	5,327	6,018
Angaur Area	406	6	420	482
Tobi Area	9	-	171	130
Sonsorol Area	7	-	153	-
Pulo Anna	-	-	19	-
6. Guam Administrative Unit:				
Guam Island Area	(1,444)		20,899	22,783

TABLE I, cont.

	1935 Japanese	1935 Foreigners	1935 Natives	1946[c] Natives[d]
7. Rota Administrative Unit:				
Rota Island Area	4,841	3	764	862
8. Saipan Administrative Unit:				
Saipan Island Area	20,280	10	3,282	3,795[e]
Tinian[f]	14,108	-	25	

a. Source: South Seas Statistical Yearbook, 1940, a publication in Japanese issued by the Japanese government.

b. Source: Naval Military Government and USCC.

c. Summer 1946, unless otherwise specified.

d. Natives (and native half-castes) only are included. Most Japanese were repatriated after V-J Day; those remaining in the summer of 1946 were either prisoners of war, special laborers (for example, on Angaur for phosphate mining), or were awaiting repatriation. Except for United States military and naval personnel, or civilians assigned to military and naval projects, the only "foreigners" remaining in Micronesia in summer 1946 were a few missionaries.

e. Since this figure was obtained, in the spring of 1946, the native population of Saipan has increased to 4,494 as of December 1946. Details are lacking about where these additions came from.

f. Tinian Island had no native population at the time it was visited by the Survey, but in 1949 some Chamorros were settled there. In 1935 there were 98 Japanese and 274 natives in four northern Mariana Islands.

One need under consideration here is for the Administration to take cognizance of differences existing among the various Culture Areas and of the grouping of Culture Areas into Administrative Units, when investigating economic conditions and when planning and applying specific measures of economic rehabilitation.

Another requirement is that caution must be exercised in the initiation of programs designed to change the native cultures. Micronesian cultures are not "pure" native cultures; but all of them represent more or less delicately balanced adaptations to specific sets of environmental and historical factors and could be badly unbalanced by unwise forced changes. Changes are inevitable, but must occur gradually and voluntarily.

Relations between ethnic groups in Micronesia merit special attention. There has been a tendency by the Administration to use the Chamorros as special assistants in dealing with other native groups. This has evoked strong feelings of resentment among the latter. The relations between the two groups on some islands have long been characterized by tension. The Chamorros in the Carolines are a minority group who have wielded power in excess of their relative numbers. Americans have further increased Chamorro power to the distress of the local populations. The rationale for this action has been that the Chamorros are more westernized and hence it is easier to use them as intermediaries than to deal directly with native leaders. The Carolinians are eager to be given comparable opportunities to develop and should be assigned posts of responsibility in accord with their proportion to the whole population. This will make for some difficulties at first, but native leadership on the whole is competent and responsible and will adjust quickly to its new responsibilities. The Administration will find that its proposals will elicit greater response from the native if they do not use the Chamorros as their agents in the Carolines.

Notes

1. This chapter describes the population situation as it was in the summer of 1946. Between that time and the beginning of 1949, there was a steady growth in native population throughout most of American Micronesia, accomplished in some measure by greatly improved naval medical facilities and more settled conditions of life. In addition, most Chamorros were repatriated to the northern Marianas (Tinian and Saipan).

2. See Table I for population breakdown by islands.

3. "Chamorros" are indigenes of the Marianas. Today many Chamorros live in the Carolines, while many Carolinians have settled in the Marianas.

4. Viewed from the vantage point of 1950, this paragraph requires some revision: while there appears to be no immediate danger of overpopulation on most islands, on some atolls the fine balance between size of population and extent of available land is in danger of upset.

5. As of 1949 some restrictions have been enacted against complete freedom of movement around the Trust Territory.

CHAPTER II. BASIC NEEDS AND RESOURCES

A. LAND

Land is the basic resource and foundation of Micronesian life and economy. Welfare and progress of native communities depend greatly therefore upon the attitude and policy of the Administration regarding land.

The land resources of Micronesia are limited. The total land area amounts to less than a thousand square miles, which has to support a native population of some 73,000. This population is unevenly distributed, so that the population density is rather high in some areas and relatively low in others. Land is not only limited in amount but also in productivity because of rugged terrain and low soil fertility.

Native concepts of land ownership differ from area to area. Under the typical pattern of land tenure in aboriginal days, village sites and fields and gardens around villages belonged to certain families or other kinship groups, while land not continually utilized, such as forest land, was owned collectively by the community.

Today these concepts range all the way from private property, as we know it, to clan ownership. The concept of land as private property is found mainly in the most acculturated sections of Micronesia, such as the Marianas, while elsewhere land is usually held by groups of individuals linked by kinship ties. In other instances, as in the Marshalls or Ponape, chiefs exercise a great deal of authority over land, so that persons not familiar with native land tenure mistakenly consider them the sole owners or landlords.

The Japanese in Micronesia assumed the attitude that only those lands which are actually used continuously are covered by valid native titles while the remainder of the land is public domain and state property which may be alienated to immigrant groups. This policy enabled the Japanese to establish agricultural settlements of their own nationals in the Marianas, the Palaus, and Ponape. In the eyes of the Micronesians there exists no no-man's land. Even the virgin forest territory in the interior of an island is claimed by and belongs to a community or a chief. The Japanese disregard of such claims has been greatly resented by the Micronesians and now that the Japanese settlers and development companies are gone the Micronesians are wondering what the American attitude regarding these lands will be. They are anxious to obtain renewed title to these lands, which have been greatly increased in value as a result of Japanese development.

Questions of land tenure are bound to cause a great many controversies and to occupy considerable time and energy of administrators in the future. Now that the Japanese administrators are gone, and with them most of the records on land ownership, old land feuds are being revived and conflicting claims presented to the new Administration.

The younger people are less familiar with the native land-tenure concepts than the older generation, which still remembers the customs observed prior to the coming of the Germans. During both the German and Japanese periods new concepts came in and land took on a new importance. It became the source of cash income since its products could be exported.

One of the most important questions to be settled is the disposal of those lands which the Japanese declared government land and opened to Japanese immigrants. On the island of Babelthuap, for example, the Japanese declared land in the interior to be state land, and they opened this land to settlement by immigrants. Now the native communities of Babelthuap desire that the land be returned to the *klobak,* or council of the chiefs. The *klobak* in turn would distribute the land among the villages which formerly claimed it. The villages would then lease the land to individuals who are interested in the development and continued exploitation of holdings improved by Japanese settlers.

In a number of instances the Military Commanders show very little concern for the land needs of native communities. On Peleliu the American armed forces occupy much of the best land – more than appears justified by their number and military requirements – and have shunted the population into less desirable districts. The population is prevented from growing its staple crop, since the armed forces claim the only remaining taro lands on the island.[1]

Some examples from Truk will indicate how native welfare has been needlessly sacrificed because of unknowing or arbitrary administrative actions. The people of Fono (Falo) Island were removed from their island because of the anticipated need for a naval recreation area. The villagers of Machitiu are prevented from returning to the old village site although their land is no longer needed by the forces. During the summer of 1946 the Commanding Officer there ordered the establishment of a leper colony, and, without consideration of the economic effect, the reef island of Sanat was selected for the site. The food production capacity of Sanat greatly exceeds the food requirements of the few lepers who are isolated on the island, but the original owners of the island are no longer permitted to attend to their property and to harvest their produce. Experience in other parts of the tropics shows that it is not absolutely necessary to select an uninhabited island as site for a leper colony. It would have been sufficient to set aside an isolated section of one of the larger inhabited islands, possibly a peninsula, or an island smaller than Sanat. That would reduce the loss of income from copra to a minimum. The chiefs of Truk should have been asked to select the site for the leper colony, taking into consideration the land requirements of the colony.

On the island of Guam leaders of the community feel that in too many instances the Navy has taken possession of land best suited to native use, leaving only inaccessible land to the Guamians – land which the Navy has the funds and the equipment to open up and develop but which is of little value to the local population because of its location.

Saipan islanders live in the war-born village of Chalan Canoa (Charan Kanoa), the former Japanese sugar-mill town. Only a few native families lived in this town before the war, having formerly lived mostly in Garapan, where they owned their own property. Many natives also own land in various other parts of the island. They want their land back again, or its equivalent. No constructive action, other than taking individual statements of land ownership in the fall of 1944, had been directed to the accomplishment of this end by midsummer 1946. Some Saipan islanders had been allowed to return to the land as farmers, but no attention had been given to whose land they were occupying. A golf course had been laid out on land which formerly was considered as part of the better farm land on the island.[2]

Many more examples could be given to demonstrate how the presence of our armed forces is unduly blocking the economic development of Micronesians. In view of the limited amount of land suitable for cultivation, it is absolutely essential that the demand for land on the part of the armed forces be reduced to the minimum.

The rehabilitation of the Micronesian islands could be speeded up greatly if the armed forces would determine their essential land requirements and would settle financial claims of individuals and communities as soon as possible.

The islands which possess phosphate deposits present a special problem. In most instances the exploitation of these deposits is not possible without reducing, if not completely destroying, the limited amount of good agricultural land on the island. Since all Micronesian islands require fertilizers, the exploitation of the phosphate deposits could be defended were Micronesian agriculture to benefit from it; but the phosphate is exported and permanently lost to Micronesia, leaving behind in the mining areas ruined agricultural land and a population permanently deprived of that resource.

In the light of the limited amount of land available, great care has to be taken everywhere to apply the principles of a sound conservation policy in order to prevent deterioration and waste of the land resources.

Specific recommendations with respect to land and land tenure follow:

The guiding principle of land policy must be to safeguard native land rights and land ownership, to provide every family with an equitable amount of land, and to assure community-wide access to essential land features.

Native concepts about land tenure must be regarded with respect. In order to ascertain present-day native concepts regarding land ownership, the people of each Culture Area should be required to codify these concepts after all sections of the community have had a chance to express their ideas on the subject. No attempt should be made to create uniformity of land-tenure concepts in Micronesia for the sake of convenience on the part of the administrators.

Wherever disputes arise between different groups of native society, for example, between chief and commoners as a result of the evolution of new concepts, communities should be encouraged to iron out the difficulties among themselves. Such a policy would contribute to the development of good relations between native communities and the Administration. Wherever disputes cannot thus be settled, administrators familiar with local land-tenure concepts should act as arbitrators, paying due respect to local tradition and equity.

There is an urgent need for the immediate establishment of a Land Office with branches in the major Culture Areas. This office would have the following tasks:[3]

1. Cadastral survey of all land, registration of old titles, and issuance of new titles of occupancy or ownership.[4] (It should be noted that there are native surveyors who participated in past land surveys, and who could contribute greatly in the task ahead.)
2. Disposal of lands owned formerly by the Japanese, wherever land is scarce and the local population requires it for subsistence or desires it for commercial agriculture. (It is realized that it will not be possible to make final assignments and to give titles to these lands until after the peace treaty with Japan, but there are no reasons why such lands should not be used by natives in need of land, with the understanding that final arrangements will have to wait the outcome of forthcoming treaties and international agreements.)
3. Resettlement of Micronesians who will not be able to return to their old lands because of permanent military installations.
4. Development of regulations and procedures whereby natives may use public land and, upon proof of occupancy and use over a limited number of years, acquire ownership. This applies particularly to the needs of young families in the Marianas.
5. Supervision of all land transactions between natives and between outsiders and natives. Such transactions should not become legally valid until they have been examined and properly registered.

Only persons of Micronesian ancestry, including half-castes, should have the right to buy land, either from the government or from individuals.

Outsiders should only have the right to lease government or private land for a limited number of years – never more than fifty years, preferably for shorter periods. Wherever individuals or groups of persons of Micronesian ancestry compete with outsiders for such leases, the former should be given preference. In case outsiders wish to lease private or community-controlled land, it must be made certain that the lessor has sufficient agricultural land left to satisfy his own needs.

B. AGRICULTURE AND FORESTRY[1]

1. *Resources*

The agricultural resources of Micronesia, including forestry, are relatively limited. The land area embraces a widely varying terrain of only about 900 square miles and supports a native population estimated at 73,000. No single basic agricultural condition prevails throughout. Except in the Marianas, which accounts for nearly half of the total land area and most of the best land, the agriculture has not developed very far by standards applying in the Temperate Zone.

The soils of the islands are of importance because of their effect and influence on the vegetation. The coral island soils and the volcanic island soils show marked differences.

The coral island soils are all of about the same character. The land has little height above the sea. It is formed from a sand spit on a coral reef, which has accumulated a residue of humus and vegetative debris from the coconut palms and other plants which eventually grew there. There is usually a thin layer of dense root growth a few inches below the surface, and below the root area lies sterile coral sand. The water-holding capacity of the soil and the vegetative mat is very small. Rains must come frequently to replenish the water supply in the easily drained soil. The fertility of these islands is unbalanced and low for all elements. With more abundant rainfall the vegetative growth is greater, the resultant plant residues are greater, and there is an exaggerated appearance of fertility and vegetative well-being.

On the volcanic islands the soil condition is much more complex. So long as the soils continue with good ground cover they seem to produce abundantly, but intensive cultivation would quickly deplete both their fertility and their humus content.

The possible improvement on the low islands is definitely limited by soil and water deficiencies. The volcanic islands offer deeper soils, steep slopes, heavy rainfall, and fairly thick vegetation, but soil fertility is low on all islands. In reference to agricultural crops, there is positive need for added nitrogen, phosphorus, and potassium. Irrigation was practiced in a small way only, and its extension is not now warranted.

Land should never be subject to foreclosure in settlement of debts, as in a trading store. This will prevent traders and others from encouraging customers to run up large accounts in order to acquire their land.

Military forces must limit their demands for land to an absolute minimum. The burden of proof should fall upon the Commanding Officer in each area to demonstrate the need for all lands held by the military forces. Military installations should be defined as including, among other things, all land from which natives are restricted.

Distinction should be made between private Micronesian and public property. The military forces should immediately return all Micronesian private property to the rightful owners. Where this is impossible because of proven needs (for example, military necessity), full compensation should be paid to the owners promptly. Wherever possible, compensation should be in the form of other land of equal value rather than in the form of cash payments.

Wherever military forces need land for permanent establishments, it should be bought. In other instances, land should only be leased.

Native claims for land held by the military forces should be examined by a local Review Board which should submit its decisions and all pertinent data to a Review Board in Washington, appointed by a Cabinet-level official. Membership of the latter should include a representative of the island Administration, a professional anthropologist, and a nonprofessional citizen of distinction.

Proceeding on the assumption that the Japanese observed the rules established by the Mandate Commission of the League of Nations as long as Japan was a member of the League of Nations, all transactions between Japanese and Micronesians involving native lands made since Japan left the League should be considered void. This would cover most, if not all, forced transactions resulting from Japanese defense preparations, most of which began after 1937. These lands should not be considered Japanese government property but should be returned to the former owners. Almost without exception the local communities did not receive the money which the Japanese government allegedly paid for the land. Instead, the money was placed in accounts of the South Seas Government to be used after the war.

The principles of conservation of natural resources must be observed in order to protect the foundation of Micronesian economy. Conservation programs should cover ground water, soil, forest, and wild life resources. The Japanese initiated conservation programs that should be resumed; such programs can be modified readily to meet new circumstances.

Subsistence crops consist mainly of root and tree crops, with fruits widely distributed but not very heavily used and with vegetables relatively unimportant. Of cash crops, copra is most important from the native point of view, although several others – including sugar, pineapples, tapioca, coffee, cotton, ivory nuts – have been important in the past or may assume importance in the future. Forest products, including lumber and fibers, are important from the point of view of utility and as future sources of income. Animal husbandry is necessary for native subsistence locally.

Insect pests are making inroads on the economic plants. Vegetables, especially those of the American garden type, are attractive to chewing insects of many sorts. The corn ear worm infests corn in the Marianas. The rhinoceros beetle is threatening the extinction of the coconut palms in Palau, and is unopposed at the moment. The beetle *Brontispa mariana* threatens the few palms on Saipan, Tinian, and Rota with extinction also. There is at present no known control. Other crops have serious pests; a plan of control of the insects and restoration of these valuable economic plants should be undertaken by competent technicians.[2] New insect pests are beginning to appear in Micronesia as a result of wartime activity and inadequate quarantine measures; the harmful effects they are bound to have upon Micronesian economic plants cannot yet be calculated but will certainly prove serious unless better quarantine measures are enforced. (Inadequate quarantine will undoubtedly have harmful effects upon Hawaiian and mainland agriculture as well.)

Land-use planning is receiving little or no attention at the present time because of the lack of a comprehensive program of agricultural development and conservation.

The general considerations stated above lead the Board to make the following recommendations with respect to the agricultural resources of Micronesia:

Natives' claims to the land should be settled as quickly as possible.

Land which is not intensively and continuously used for specific purposes should be planted with some crop appropriate to the terrain to prevent weeds taking possession, to prevent wind and water erosion, and to preserve the humus and soil fertility. In the high islands, consideration should be given to planting grasses, including Dallis grass, Guinea grass, and Napier grass, and good legumes like tropical kudzu, creeping indigo, and wild tamarind. In the case of any lack of decision about use to be made of arable land, such land should be put into some crop which will prevent erosion, build the soil, offer grazing for cattle, and lower insect populations.

Revegetation of denuded areas will have to proceed according to a plan of nature. Revegetation begins with the reëstablishment of the indigenous herbs and vines, and shrubs to give a ground cover, as soon as possible. This protection keeps down the soil temperature, preserves humus, prevents rapid evaporation loss after rains, and permits the planting of coconuts and other economic plants under more favorable circumstances. Denuded atolls may be reclaimed in this way – slowly, it is true. Abandoned airstrips present a special problem.

Airstrips were constructed on many islands, often laid down on land which was primarily valuable for agricultural purposes. Many airstrips are now totally abandoned. The problem is how to return these sites to economic use. Frequently, an airstrip was built far enough inland to have covered ground which formerly caught fresh water that supplied taro swamps and breadfruit growth. The construction material of the airstrip was commonly coral debris hauled from the lagoon by dragline methods and filled into the area to sufficient depth to supply a solid and level foundation for airplane landing. The low ground was more deeply filled, and the taro swamps covered with the maximum depth of coral rock and sand. The rolling of the fill incident to construction, and the cementing nature of the coral saturated with sea water, has provided a structure not easily removed or destroyed. It would be a major operation and expense to assemble machinery and personnel to uncover the land, by removing the fill. The reclaimed land would be worthless agriculturally for a considerable time, if not permanently. A new soil composed of organic residues and mineral constituents would need to be built up over a painfully long time.

If absolutely essential, small pits might be recovered for the growing of taro, but at great expense. With patience and skillful management, coconuts might be induced to grow on some of these sites. For the most part, however, agricultural land destroyed by the construction of airstrips must be regarded as one of the casualties of war.

Control of coconut palm insects should be studied with the end in view of restoring the palm in the Palaus and Marianas where it is threatened with extinction. With a source of infestation in the area, it is reasonable to believe that spread of the insects to new areas will almost surely occur. The various pests, including insects, snails, and rodents, which are making inroads on native economic crops throughout the islands, are probably too well established to be eradicated by dusts or sprays or poisons within the means of the natives to acquire or apply; the Administration should assume the responsibility of seeking less expensive biological control measures and of instituting more effective quarantine controls.

Because of its paramount importance in many native communities, selections of the breadfruit tree should be made for propagation and increase in those islands where it grows poorly, with small yield of fruit or timber. The diseased condition of the tree, so obvious in many islands, deserves study with the end in view of restoring it to health and productivity.

Soil fertility is low throughout Micronesia and should be increased by whatever means is expedient. The mineral fertilizers are low, the soils needing nitrogen, phosphorous, and potassium, and doubtless some of the minor elements. The stock of phosphate earth in the area should be reserved for use by Micronesians.

Forest promotion on marginal land, not suited to agriculture, should be undertaken in due time. The subject should be studied with the purpose of developing a reserve of choice timber and cabinet woods for future subsistence and income needs.

Investigation of agricultural problems by qualified personnel, supplied with experimental land and equipment, is necessary for an adequate understanding of land and crop problems, disease and insect control, forestry, and stability of agriculture generally. The extension of agricultural information to the natives will promote their welfare and security.

2. *Subsistence*

Food is the first concern of the Micronesian. The principal native occupation is focused on food procurement and its preparation. Food is a pleasure to them as well as sustenance and takes on in part the character of medicine, health being related to the choice and supply of food available.

The kinds and nature of the food plants are greatly restricted by type and availability of the soil, by amount and quality of soil water, by proximity of the salt water beach, and by climatic features. The combined handicap permits only a few perennials to grow well. Little is grown which is of an annual or short-season habit. Yet, over centuries of time the natives have survived, if not prospered, on these few food plants.

New species have been introduced from time to time, but are rated as less valuable than the few fundamental plants carried down from the remote past.

Although natives are dependent principally upon plant foods, their diets also include fish and other sea food, pork and other meat, fowl, and some imported items. These provide the principal protein element of the diet and some valuable vitamin constituents.

The quantity of food is usually ample but seldom excessive. There is little opportunity for creating a reserve or for holding one for a very long time. Most of the plant products are perishable, the chief exceptions being corn and prepared tapioca flour, which are limited to some of the high islands.

Cooking is required for practically all of the food except a few fruits. Cooking and exposure result in some loss of minerals and vitamins, but the staple starches have to be cooked to become digestible. Flavors of prepared native foods are monotonous, consistency bland, and variety small; they have very little appeal to the American palate.

Some islanders have learned to accept and like introduced foods, but all natives cling to many elements of the old diets. The coconut meat and milk from both green and mature nuts furnish universal and constant ingredients added in some way to nearly every dish. Breadfruit is seasonal and of prime importance while it lasts. Taro, of many varieties, has been the largest single tended crop and, with breadfruit, a principal source of starch. Arrowroot is a tuber-like root of a small plant which grows well under coconut palms and is regarded as a reserve food rather than one of first choice. The banana is eaten as fresh fruit or cooked (plantain), there being many varieties. Pandanus fruit segments are chewed for the tasteful juice of the pulp, or the sections are sometimes roasted. Squash or gourds are commonly found. Chamorros cultivate a white dent corn, a plant which must have been introduced by the Spanish. The Tahitian chestnut is grown and relished in Yap, the Palaus, and in the southern Marshalls.

The Japanese introduced new plants and forced their culture, especially manioc (the root) or tapioca (the starch). Imported rice has come to be regarded as almost a necessity among most communities. Soya sauce is also highly regarded and is used to flavor the otherwise flat foods. Canned beef is in demand almost everywhere. Flour and yeast for breadmaking, or flour alone, are regarded as necessities by Chamorros and Marshallese. Other imports desired by natives are canned fish, sugar, table salt, tea, pepper, dry biscuits, and canned milk.

Vegetables are not grown by the Marshallese, but the Chamorros and natives of Palau grow beans, soya, daikon, turnips, Chinese cabbage, and a few other vegetable items. Yams are long established on Ponape. Sweet potatoes are accepted by the Yap natives, but are not popular elsewhere.

Fruits are not utilized as fully as they might or should be. The papaya is not usually liked by natives and in many places is wholly neglected. Pineapples are grown in small numbers usually as individual plants. Limes, mandarins, oranges, lemons, and a small tangerine are found growing throughout the islands and are eaten now and then.

Livestock resources are small. The Japanese consumed the majority of the livestock in many islands during the war years. The present animal census is not known for all localities, but it is established that it is at a very low point. Formerly, pigs and chickens were well distributed, and the average Chamorro family usually possessed a cow.

An estimate of livestock needs may be based on the count of families in the islands. Each family so desiring should possess a cow, where land which will support the cow is operated by the family. This assignment is necessarily confined to the high islands.

Pigs were formerly well distributed throughout Micronesia on both high and low islands. To restore pork, the most beneficial meat of any locally produced, to the native diet, two pigs per family could well be the goal. The pigs gain weight slowly because of feed type and shortage and are killed at weight less than the American optimum. In the low islands feed may not be sufficient to support and fatten two pigs per family, a factor which will influence distribution and increase. It is not feasible to distribute pigs immediately in quantity sufficient to provide for each family as recommended. Bred sows of grade quality, with a boar of grade quality or better for service in the local area, should provide for steady increase and attainment of the goal within two or three years. Until the pig population can be increased, there will remain a continued shortage of meat for subsistence.

Each family should have chickens up to the quantity they desire and can feed. The increase in chickens is slow in the islands. Eggs for setting and hens for hatching are required in each place. Large-scale hatchery methods are not now feasible.[3]

Both pigs and poultry should have feeds and concentrates for steady growth and optimum development. Both are subject to diseases and parasites. Health and nutrition of animals is an important factor in their increase and supply in the native economy and will tend to be a limiting factor, if not a controlling one, in building up the animal population.

Such is the general picture. There are, however, many differences among the separate areas.

The Marshallese diet centers around coconut, breadfruit, taro, pandanus, a few bananas when they can get them, and arrowroot; pork, chicken, and fish - with the pork and chicken reserved for feasts. They are anxious to be supplied with rice, flour, canned meat and fish, sugar, and salt. By contact with Americans they are beginning to like coffee, cheese, bread, and other foods served natives in labor-camp messes.

Eastern Caroline dietary habits vary widely between the large islands of Kusaie and Ponape, where a large and varied food supply is available, and the small islands which are limited to bare essentials of coconut, taro, pandanus, breadfruit, arrowroot, and fish. These latter islands are infrequently visited and in the past have had little or nothing to trade. Being extremely poor, they are hardly able to purchase on the outside and largely lack the necessities of fish hooks, good knives, and cotton cloth, and the luxury of rice, sugar, and canned goods.

The natives of Truk are similar to those of the other high islands in their general food habits. Their resources include the wide variety of foods found on the high islands, both in staples, fruit, and the introduced plants of manioc and sugar cane. The possibility of increase of quantity is good, and of diversification excellent. There is a real shortage of pigs and chickens, and steps toward restoration of this animal population should begin. The native diet appears to be reasonably well fixed in food preferences.

Some western Caroline islands are moderately well supplied with food and follow the usual native pattern with coconuts, breadfruit, taro, pandanus, pigs, and fish. Before the war, the large island of Yap was well off in food plants, especially taro and Chamorro corn, in cattle, and in pigs and chickens. The Yap native clings to a regimen different from that of the Chamorro. Yap natives have been diminishing in numbers at an alarming rate, but it is not demonstrated that diet is the cause.

The Palaus have been devastated by combat and their resources are momentarily low. The diet was formerly more varied and included beef, milk, pork, fowl, and fish, both fresh and dried. The large numbers of resident Japanese swayed the natives somewhat to their diet pattern, including rice, vegetables, and fruit.

The Mariana Chamorros have a diet of coconut, corn, breadfruit, taro, sweet potato, rice, cassava, citrus, vegetables, and have a history of using beef, pork, milk, fowl, eggs, and fish.

The Polynesian natives of the southern-lying islands of Kapingamarangi and Nukuoro have a diet of coconut, taro, breadfruit, bananas, pork, fowl, and fish.

There is no marked distinction between the nutritional condition of the various native groups, although there is some slight difference between the dietary conditions of natives according to whether they live in the poorer low islands or on the richer, more productive high islands. Most natives appear to have a sufficient quantity of food, but it is not well balanced, and the reserve is small.

The Survey nutritional specialist examined a number of island native groups for general health with reference to the nutritional deficiency syndrome. Severe cases of under-nutrition resulting in definite deficiency disease were not found. Tissue changes of eye parts, skin, mouth, and contour were examined for indication of vitamin and nutritional sufficiency. Teeth were generally good. Natives' high carbohydrate diet should be, but is not, compensated by a higher-than-average vitamin level of intake. They suffer from such diseases as yaws, bacterial infections, intestinal parasites, and fungus infestations. Tuberculosis is a common and primary cause of death. The level of nutrition is important to the native because of the relation of it to the other types of disease. Malnutrition is the most important predisposing factor for their list of infectious diseases, including tuberculosis, yaws, or any which are chronic.

The adults were found to be fairly well developed, the males especially so; but the children had an appearance younger than seemed to agree with their stated ages. Many were underweight and scrawny. It must be remembered, however, that most of the children were born and reared during the deprivation and stringency of the war years. During the war, natives' pigs and chickens were taken by the Japanese, fishing was prohibited or destroyed by dynamiting and loss of boats. These protein sources have not been restored in prewar proportions, and children more than others have been deprived of their lifetime share of protein foods.

By some means the islands should be restocked initially with pigs, chickens, and ducks, and, where warranted, with cattle and goats. The animal protein is low in quantity or absent and cannot be restored quickly enough with the stock in hand. Crop plants are generally sufficient, or could soon be made so, for the need they supply.

It is not anticipated that major changes in native diets can be brought about easily, and there is insufficient evidence that such is desirable if the basic food supply is again restored to normal. Some of the nutritional deficiencies could be partly corrected, at least, by better use and attention to the food resources at hand. Increase by reproduction of animals after distribution should be persistently urged until a backlog of breeding stock is assured. Crop plants should remain principally within the traditional range for the present. The aim then will be to insure ample production, a principal concern, and to increase quality with mineral and vitamin content. Micronesia should be self-sufficient in basic foods, enjoying an ample and nutritionally balanced diet.

Specific recommendations for restoring prewar diet standards are given below:

An effort should be made to insure a safe margin of supply over need, by building up a greater backlog of unused food-crop plants. Coconuts, breadfruit, taro, pandanus, and arrowroot should be increased and maintained in the low islands in excess of subsistence requirements.

In the low islands efforts to produce fruit should continue, with reference to banana and plantain, pineapple, papaya, citrus, Tahitian chestnut, and such vegetables as the natives will accept.

In the high islands subsistence-crop plants should be developed and diversified as for the low islands, with the addition of crops which will grow there, such as corn, manioc, sweet- and soursop, Eugenia fruit, Jack fruit, citrus, and others, to the end that these islands become self-sufficient in regard to food plants.

Both the high and low islands need to be restocked and replenished with pigs and chickens, the first objective being to assist each family to possess at least two pigs and chickens up to the limit of available feed. In the high islands an opportunity should be afforded for each family to possess a cow, in addition to pigs and chickens as recommended above.

No recommendation is being made regarding supply of bullocks or carabao for farm draft animals or tractive power on the farm. The Chamorro practice of using the cow or bullock may continue, and as secondary to the use of the animal for meat.

The order of importance of animals for food is: pigs, chickens, cows, ducks, and goats. The goat should be sparingly allocated owing to its destructive habits.

Pigs should be acclimated to local conditions as far as possible, and use should be made of the existing native stock where available. The Berkshire and Hampshire breeds seem to prevail in the islands and should continue. Bred sows should be distributed with the idea of increase and further distribution until the goal is reached. A breeding program using boars of good record should be undertaken.

Chickens of the heavy breeds should be selected for distribution in the islands. Poultry can be increased by supplying eggs for setting and hatching. Chickens should be increased up to the safe limit of food supply available to poultry.

Cows for milk as well as meat will be allocated to the high islands, mostly in the Marianas and in Palau. Acclimated stock, bred if possible for increase, should be available for distribution in limited numbers.

Vegetables are now no factor in low islands, but as the agriculture becomes better understood some selections of species or strain and new methods may make limited vegetable growing possible. It is recommended that efforts toward vegetable growing be extended, and in spite of the present native resistance to a vegetable diet. In the high islands a study of vegetable growing should be undertaken for both the benefit of the native and the American section of the population.

Hand tools are required in amounts necessary to provide each native with one or more. A knife of good quality steel and adapted to the prevailing need of the user, such as a copra knife, machete, butcher knife, or any general utility knife, is indispensable. A knife of good quality steel is particularly emphasized.

On the high islands where plowing is customarily done, simple plows of the type used by the Chamorro are required. In addition to the tools named above, they will need adzes, shovels, hoes, mattocks, and similar tools.

Grindstones, which were formerly used by the natives, are needed on all islands.

Blacksmith equipment should be supplied where competent natives are found who can fashion tools, knives, and such special devices as are required for the island economy and as can be made of materials at hand.

C. FISHING

Fish and shellfish are the most important sources of protein in the native diet, supplying also minerals and vitamins essential to health and well-being. Other protein foods, such as chickens, hogs, coconut crabs, and fruit bats are generally so scarce that they are reserved for feasts and special occasions. Fisheries products, on the other hand, are abundant in both number and variety. Shellfish, including marine snails, clams, spiny lobsters, and a host of others, can be taken by hand on the flat reefs near shore, and here also men use throw nets and beach seines on smooth sections, while women and girls surround small fish with hand nets. Reef fish of many species are common both within and without the lagoons and are taken with hook and line, by diving and spearing, in stone traps measuring two hundred yards across and woven basket traps lifted by hand. Outside the reefs, crevallé, bonito, and barracuda are taken by trolling, and flying fish are caught in scoop nets at night, attracted by coconut-leaf torches. Every able-bodied man, woman, and child usually spends some part of each day fishing.

Daily consumption of fish products is high. If it can be obtained, some kind of fish is served with each meal, and estimates made by natives at many different places agree on a figure of a pound per person per day. This rate of production is not being met everywhere. At Rota, Guam, Koror, Yap, Truk, and Ponape, supplies are below needs. On Rota the reef area is relatively small with no offshore fishing. Fish will probably always occupy a less important place in the diet there than other proteins. On Guam, labor requirements of the armed services doubtless always will provide more work under better conditions, and few persons will be fishermen.

In the Palaus, the Japanese destroyed all but 80 of the 1500 native canoes, thus wiping out nearly all fishing activities. As boatbuilding gets underway, however, the fishing fleets should quickly rectify the temporary shortages of sea food. On the main islands of the Truk group, where the Japanese population was located, food shortages during the war caused the Japanese to use dynamite and hand grenades to take quantities of fish from the reefs, the fish population being greatly reduced thereby. It will be several years before natural reproduction will bring the supply back to normal. A similar situation exists at Ponape, though the destruction of fish was not as great as at Truk. With the exceptions noted, it is generally the case that resources are more than ample to meet native needs, but it is necessary to see that local supplies of fishing gear are provided immediately and maintained in sufficient quantity.

Methods of preparation are varied, but ordinarily no seasoning is used. Some fish and most bivalves such as clams are eaten raw. The custom of marinating raw fish with lime juice is common. Baking on hot stones and boiling are the most frequently used methods of cooking. Frying in coconut oil is less common, except in the Marianas, and is generally limited to minnows or young fish of small size. Turtles are roasted in their own shells.

In considering native requirements for fishing equipment and supplies, it is necessary to distinguish between the relatively simple needs of the atoll population and the larger demands of high islands, especially the more heavily populated islands of Saipan, Guam, the Palaus, and Ponape. On the latter islands, labor is more specialized because of large economic demands. Many persons are regularly employed full time as farmers, carpenters, and in other occupations for the armed forces and civilians. They must therefore purchase many of their foods instead of personally collecting them.

On the atolls, the main needs are for fishhooks, feather jigs, metal spoons, fishing lines, seine twine, steel rod for spears, and a small amount of marine hardware.

On the high islands mentioned, such items must be supplemented with commercial fishing gear. For example, the 4500 natives on Saipan cannot be supplied with fishery products through individual use of fishing gear. Production from the 1946 fishing fleets is not sufficient to supply the demand. For the places mentioned, adequate fishing equipment includes not only diesel-powered vessels and refrigeration space, but also such maintenance and operation items as marine ways, motor and hull repair facilities, and docks and processing installations, with trained personnel to take care of them.[1]

D. HOUSING

Restoration of shelter facilities, necessitated by population dislocation and destruction of housing during the war, has become a top priority problem of rehabilitation everywhere in the islands. As one native on Yap said in summing up the present inadequacies of life, "If we could have homes again, everything else would work out in time."

Wherever the Japanese built military bases on native village sites, families were compelled to seek new homes. Some natives crowded into existing housing with relatives in other islands, some were pushed back into the hills and to other undeveloped areas where they improvised crude shacks or sought cover within dank caves. Native laborers, recruited by the Japanese to level airstrips and construct concrete pillboxes, were quartered in huge barracks hastily thrown together for their use, while their families had to keep up the homesteads without the help of their menfolk. During the last few years of the war, Japanese soldiers on by-passed islands and atolls dispossessed native families from housing erected by the latter in peacetime and dismantled the frame dwellings to salvage lumber, hardware, and iron roofing for their own needs.

American strafing and bombing wrought untold damage to native villages and to more densely populated towns like Garapan, Agaña, Koror, and Ponape Colonia; some of these raids preceded actual invasions, while others were practice runs for the sake of training new pilots from the mainland. After Kwajalein, Angaur, Saipan, and Guam were invaded, native refugees were brought in from other islands and from the hills where they had sought cover from roving Japanese troops. Military Government teams settled them in camps, like Chalan Canoa on Saipan, where the exigencies of the war which was still raging about them dictated only a minimum satisfaction of human living requirements - too many families in too few houses, inadequate sanitary facilities, constant regimentation, and no privacy for family life. On Guam and other islands, the American military required additional acreage for bomber-strips and warehouses and barracks, so once more the natives were relocated in less desirable areas in temporary housing. All of this took place under conditions of war, when winning battles was more essential than rehabilitating native populations. Now the war is over and the time has come to survey realistically the true condition of native housing and other population needs in terms of what concrete measures can be taken to correct existing inadequacies.

For the islands as a whole, perhaps 50 per cent of prewar native-occupied housing was modified Japanese or European in style and construction; but outside of Guam, the rest of the Marianas, and parts of the Palaus, the traditional dwelling of Micronesia was more prevalent - a rectangular, one-family affair, with thatched and gabled roof, a raised floor, and low walls. In the low coral atolls, native huts are more often built directly on the ground and the earthen floor is covered with a layer of coral pebbles and woven mats. Wherever the floor is raised several feet off the ground on wood, stone, or concrete foundations, the open space beneath is utilized as storage, for keeping pigs and chickens, or as a place to work on hot or rainy days. In the western Carolines wooden ladders or steps lead from the ground to entrances at the floor level of the dwellings and there is considerable ornamentation of clubhouse timbers, which are painted, carved, or decorated with shellwork, a characteristic entirely lacking in the Marshalls. Timbers are generally mortised at the joints or lashed together with sennit. Sides of dwellings may be open or walled with thatch, woven reeds, bamboo, splints of wood, or plaited mats of coconut and pandanus leaf; openings at intervals admit light and air, but can be covered with mats and screens during inclement weather. Flooring of bamboo poles or planks of native hardwoods are characteristic. The roofs are thatched with leaves of pandanus, coconut, nipa, or ivory-nut palm trees. Most materials needed in construction, such as wood for timbers and flooring, leaves for thatch, stone for foundations, and bamboo or reeds for wall coverings, can be obtained from local resources.

Details of construction, style, and ornamentation vary considerably from one island group to another. Generally, one family comprises a household, but close relatives may be included; there are five to ten occupants per dwelling as a rule. The dwellings of chiefs and other natives of high social status are larger, better built, and more favorably located within the settlement. The average one-room house is enlarged in the western islands to two or more rooms, mat or reed partitions dividing the floor area according to local demands. House construction is usually a community project, many hands making short work of an otherwise long and laborious task. Relatives pool their labor to finish the project in a few days, celebrating its completion with feasting, song, and dancing. Men are always responsible for the heavier work with stone and timbers, while women furnish thatch and matting.

Although the aboriginal dwelling prevails throughout most of the islands, the past two decades have been characterized by a definite trend toward a modified Japanese or European style in architecture and the use of modern building materials. Wooden houses with iron roofs were fairly common before the war for families of chiefs, half-castes, and other prominent individuals in native communities. In areas where Japanese and Okinawan settlements set the example, the adoption by natives of western housing was quite prevalent. In Guam and the Marianas, natives had forsaken their traditional housing to the greatest extent; more than half of Chamorro dwellings were roofed with iron, all were substantially built with wood siding and flooring, and some had concrete floors and walls and glazed windows. Yap has been most backward in adopting modern housing, a resistance which characterizes Yap in other aspects of culture as well. Even the Japanese government program, which subsidized native houses built with raised floors, iron roofs, and doors and windows, received little consideration by the natives of Yap. In general, it may be assumed that modified western construction has become established in native minds as the most desirable type of shelter. Wooden frame dwellings with concrete floors and iron roofs may be hotter than the native thatched hut, but they are more permanent (native thatch must be renewed every three or four years, and timbers replaced every ten years or less); they are cleaner, not collecting rats and insects in the thatch or soiling clothes with dirt from earthen floors; they can better withstand earthquake and typhoon, a factor to be seriously considered in the western islands; and the iron roof provides an excellent means for rain water catchment, one of the major sources of potable water supply.

Furniture in native houses is extremely limited, except where the western influence has ordained otherwise. Sleeping mats and cooking utensils of wood and metal have been supplemented by kerosene lanterns, wooden storage chests, and sewing machines. Even tables, chairs, bedsteads, mirrors, and phonographs are not uncommon in more modern homes.

All cooking is carried on separately from the dwelling house, although in some areas the thatched shelter which serves as cookhouse may be attached to the rear of the dwelling. The cookhouse is built on the ground, with an earth oven or a hearth of three upright stones at one end, the smoke from the fire finding its way out through an open side or the loosely built roof.

Outdoor toilet facilities are nearly universal in the islands. Only Guam and Saipan boast indoor plumbing in the better homes. The Japanese *benjo,* located at some distance from the dwelling or on piles over the water, has replaced the native custom of relieving oneself on the outer shore at low tide. Menstrual huts, set apart from the living area for the seclusion of menstruating or parturient women, were once common throughout the islands, but have generally disappeared in these times, except on Yap. Bathing is an informal matter in most areas, the people using streams and pools, which are also used for washing clothes. However, in missionized areas like the Marshalls, the Palaus, and the Marianas, special facilities are erected so that one may bathe in private under a shower or in a tub of water.

Today, many natives have already been repatriated to their old village sites and are hard at work to reëstablish themselves. Others remain in crowded camps or in mountain refuges for lack of better facilities. In the Marshalls, where Americans have had control for nearly three years, the housing situation is still far from satisfactory; but in other areas, such as Truk, Ponape, and Palau, where Japanese garrisons surrendered only a year ago, practically nothing has been done to ameliorate housing conditions, because of the inadequacy of building supplies and lack of organization on the part of Military Government offices. Everywhere the natives are faced with shortages of construction materials and labor.[1]

Native resources, such as pandanus, coconut, and various timber trees, have been destroyed or sharply curtailed in islands which were devastated by the war. Lumber, sheet-iron roofing, and other modern materials have been salvaged by some natives who have been fortunate enough to have access to demolished Japanese bases and evacuated Okinawan settlements. In some cases, surplus stocks from American military installations have been put at the disposal of needy families for rebuilding homes. Whenever the supply of materials has been completely inadequate to the existing need, makeshift housing of a squalid and unsanitary sort has resulted. Canvas tents are a common sight in many villages. In the two places where a surplus of housing exists – on Peleliu and Angaur, where native families are quartered in well-furnished Quonset huts – the natives lack title to their homes and stand in danger of being dispossessed at any time if the military decides to use the Quonsets for another purpose. This matter of titles to houses and to the land on which structures have been built is a common problem in islands where the military was forced by the demands of war to get the natives under shelter at once and resorted to temporary housing erected in available locations regardless of land ownership. As a result, these families cannot improve their dwellings because they have no permanent claim on improved facilities and will be moved when land titles are eventually cleared.

Labor is dear in the sense that housing is only one of the many time-consuming occupations which face the people: gardens and plantations to clean up and cultivate, daily food supply to secure, boats and canoes to be built or reconditioned, roads to maintain, and copra and handicraft to produce for trade-goods exchange. In a few instances the Administration has unfortunately required all available native manpower for work on quasi-military projects, which has prevented the normal resumption of village activities or the completion of housing requirements.

Specific recommendations for housing are as follows:

Construction of native housing should be given the highest priority, along with food relief, as being the most pressing need in the rehabilitation of island peoples. In the allocation of funds available for rehabilitation, private housing should receive primary consideration. Where natives need financial assistance to restore prewar facilities, subsidies should be provided by the Administration. Eventually native claims for war damages will be submitted for compensation, but their needs are immediate and cannot wait for settlement at the peace table.

The problem of land titles should be investigated with the view of resettling every native family on its own land or, where return is impossible, making adjustment by the allocation of comparable acreage elsewhere. This clearance of land titles should be given a high priority and proceed concurrently with housing reconstruction, in order to allow the maximum use of building materials presently available and to return native communities to normal as soon as possible.[2]

For permanent housing, natives in many areas need scantlings, boards or plywood for siding, cement for foundations, flooring, walls, and cisterns, corrugated iron roofing, galvanized iron eaves-trough and rain pipe, house paint, nails, screws, hinges, and glass for windows. All building materials which are imported or otherwise made available for native use should be invested in permanent shelter and not be wasted in temporary construction. Previous construction undertaken by the Administration was temporary by necessity; the emergency is now past and considered planning should replace improvisation. Building materials are, and will continue to be, difficult to obtain for native needs, and every precaution must be taken to conserve the stocks which are on hand and use them to best advantage as part of a long-range program for housing.

Where such has not been done already, all surplus building supplies at abandoned or reduced American military bases in the islands should be made available to needy natives for private housing. If necessary, provision should be made to furnish transportation to distribute these supplies among the population.

In the same way, wherever Japanese barracks and other installations exist in the islands, every effort should be made to salvage whatever lumber, roofing, and other usable materials remain and to distribute them among the local native population for housing construction.

Good quality tools - hammers, saws, planes, drills, squares, rules - are in insufficient quantity in the islands for the building program which lies ahead and should be made available to natives who know how to use and care for them.

In some of the high islands, sawmills should be reconditioned and put into operation for processing surplus local timber resources, with due concern for conservation requirements. In general, the principle should prevail that immediate housing needs be filled with imported supplies, while local resources are allowed to increase for fulfillment of future needs. Wherever reforestation will aid in building up local reserves of timber and other resources, proper measures should be instituted.

A special study should be made of housing conditions throughout the islands, with attention given to local resources and requirements in each area. At least one administrative officer in each area should be assigned responsibility for native housing, the efforts of these field officers being coördinated by a housing specialist attached to the administrative staff at Guam or Honolulu.

Serious consideration should be given to supplying furniture and furnishings as requested by many natives who were already well accustomed to them prior to the war – tables, chairs, chests, kerosene lamps, bedsteads, blankets, metal utensils and cutlery, plates, cups, glasses, can openers, charcoal braziers, sewing machines, and phonographs. It can no longer be argued that these are "luxury items" and "nonessential to the primitive needs of simple natives."

E. GOODS: CONSUMER, DURABLE, PRODUCTIVE, AND CAPITAL

Present-day consumption levels in Micronesia are far below those which prevailed before the war.[1] The decline in standard of living was brought about by a whole complex of factors: the cessation of Japanese imports for native use after the war started; the heavy use of native supplies by the Japanese military; the destruction of native property and resources during combat; the depletion of supply reserves; the loss of the capital equipment for the manufacture of articles; the consumption of breeding livestock; the withdrawal of natives from subsistence activities; the breakdown of the distribution system; the emphasis of the present Administration on granting assistance only of the emergency type for making survival possible; the devaluation of the yen and the restriction to a small fraction of their prewar holdings the amount of money natives were permitted to keep; the disappearance of their savings; the low purchasing power of money currently earned; the restriction in opportunities for gaining a regular income from service enterprises, from the sale of exportable goods, and from employment; the paucity of American imports to replace that which had been lost.

As a consequence, the native populations are impoverished. Every island now suffers from an acute shortage of essential items, many of which cannot be produced locally. Without these the natives are unable even to use effectively their local resources for subsistence. No group faces starvation, but none has enough supplies to make possible the restoration of the economy to the point where it can function as it once did and could do once more. No one is totally lacking in shelter, but few have the kind of homes and household utensils which they possessed before the war. No one is without clothing, and yet there is a widespread demand for fabrics to make clothes like those formerly worn.

The presence or absence of imported goods means to most natives the difference between a satisfactory standard of living and a submarginal one, the difference between having a chance to become self-sufficient through their own production or being dependent upon the government for relief, the difference between progressing toward a better life or recession to the kind of life which existed in aboriginal times.

The extent of basic native requirements varies in magnitude more than in kind among the islands. Palau and Saipan natives require much more to equal their prewar conditions than do those in Yap and Truk. But the most significant fact is that all are in need. The scarcities have been listed in detail for each of the islands in the individual "subject" reports.[2] It will be noted that throughout Micronesia the current demands far exceed the supplies now available.

In the prewar period, all of the islands of Micronesia received a variety of imports from abroad. The Japanese provided a wide range of low-priced goods at regular intervals and extended the trade to the most remote atolls. The quality of the manufactured articles was not high; the natives deem the items inferior to those offered by the Germans in the preceding period and below American products in durability. But they were designed for local conditions and the needs of the local populations. Thus, finished clothes were of the weight most suitable for the climate and were made in sizes which fitted native statures. Consumer goods were sold at prices which were geared to native earning powers. In addition, the Japanese subsidized the natives in the procurement of capital and durable goods beyond their financial resources.

Because of the multiplicity of local needs for imports and the limited capacity to provide them at this time, all supplies to be sent to Micronesia should be chosen with care for greatest practical use.

For the present, because of world shortages in some commodities, no special effort should be made to obtain such items except in cases of demonstrated emergency need. Eventually it will work out that local import requirements can be geared into the world supply situation without special efforts. During the emergency period, imports should be selected to get in only essential supplies. Production and consumer durable goods should be given first priority: tools and implements needed to gain a subsistence, livestock for breeding, construction materials, household utensils, and textiles should receive the heaviest emphasis in procurement and distribution.

Until the goods are put on the islands where they are needed, they are unfilled orders. Supplies allocated on paper and lists of requisitions are not supplies usable by the natives. The two classes oftentimes have been mistakenly identified. Requisition lists from some islands have not been filled at all; others have been delayed as much as six months. Special efforts should be directed toward the movement of supplies requisitioned from their location in stockpiles to the places of actual use.

Subsistence provisioning is possible in many localities. In these the natives should be expected to assist and be assisted themselves to develop provisions to meet their maximum needs. Assistance involves the determination of land which natives can use permanently for growing their food, freeing them of other duties so that they can gain their subsistence, and providing the equipment required for making a living in Micronesia. None of these conditions now prevails. In those islands where subsistence living is not now possible, imports of consumer goods are essential until a subsistence economy can be reestablished. Thus Guam, Saipan, Wotje, Angaur, and Peleliu are not now in a condition to allow the natives to become self-sustaining. All of these islands might eventually become so if proper measures of the types indicated above are undertaken; but to require it immediately would make for acute suffering. It is the responsibility of the Administration to see that the essential needs of the natives are met.

The demand for goods can be classified into two types: (1) commodities required throughout the islands of Micronesia by all native populations; and (2) commodities required for particular areas and sections of the native populations. The use of this distinction in the procurement, stockpiling, and allocation of supplies will make for greater economy and for a more effective distribution system than now prevails. In the appraisal of the requests for class (2) items, the decisions of the field staff representatives should not be modified without their approval. In cases of differences between the field officer and the supplying agency, the matter should be referred to a higher authority. The higher authority should consider the requests of the area in terms of its prewar standard of living, the extent of destruction, the size of the population, the native customs in the use of goods, and related factors. Decisions on major issues should be made only after complete information has been assembled on these questions. The tendency has been to evaluate supply requisitions at the higher levels on the basis of inadequate data using the preconception that the Micronesians are "primitives" and hence their supplies should be confined to a few elementary articles.

Action should be taken as swiftly as possible to take an inventory of consumer needs and the local stockpiles on each of the islands. The inventory should include equipment on islands no longer occupied by the armed forces, Japanese supplies, and useful civilian materials in Navy, Army, and Marine Corps depots. The articles should be itemized in sufficient detail so that their specific usages can be appraised. Emphasis in the evaluation of supplies should be on their usefulness to the native economy rather than on their uselessness to the armed forces. The practice is common of dumping any unwanted items, regardless of their value, on the natives. In computing the cost of goods, the calculation should take into account their depreciation through prior use and weathering.

In some instances, the cost has been computed by supply officers as that of the original manufacturing price.

Upon the completion of the inventory, those supplies not required within the locality should be shipped at once to designated stockpile points. These stockpiles should be given continuous care to secure the commodities and to maintain sufficient supplies of the types in constant demand. Area administrators should be required to report at fixed and frequent intervals to higher authority the extent to which they have complied with present directives on the disposition of excess supplies for native use. Emphasis should be placed on the obligation of local administrators to fulfill these directives; in the past the directives have been interpreted as permitting the release of supplies rather than as requiring their allocation. The allocation of supplies should be established as a regular procedure to be made as often as the need arises. Some of the most unused items are rapidly disintegrating from want of care. That which is not procurable from existing stockpiles should be procured as rapidly as possible on the mainland or elsewhere.

A survey should be made to determine the supplies which can be obtained in Japan.[3] Reports from Japan indicate the existence of substantial stockpiles of the kind of goods vitally needed in Micronesia. It is urged that barter arrangements be made with SCAP so that Micronesia can trade its products, which are urgently needed in Japan, for what Micronesia wants. If the phosphate shipments to Japan must continue, the islands should receive in return manufactured goods from Japan. Shrewd bargaining is called for on behalf of the natives. Japanese manufacturers know the native markets and can meet the needs.

To the fullest extent possible, natives should be encouraged to produce or buy their own consumer goods rather than receive them without charge from the Administration. Consumer goods produced by native society for native use should be facilitated through making available capital, equipment, technical guidance, and so forth. Controls on consumer goods produced by native society should be confined to the following: (1) ceiling prices on scarce items fixed by joint decision of the Administration and native leadership; (2) inspection for enforcement of sanitation and quarantine; (3) insurance of free competition among natives.

Those capital and durable goods essential to the economy but which the natives are unable to produce or pay for should be provided by the Administration. Joint sharing of the cost by Administration and natives should be made for production goods. The unit of subsidy will depend on local conditions; the policy should be to spread ownership as far as possible within the native society rather than to set up a small monopoly for the benefit of one group. Credit should be extended to the natives for meeting their share of the cost. In the granting of credit due regard must be made of local usages, the reputation of the individuals in meeting obligations and in operating successful business enterprises, the period required for the repayment of the debt, native attitudes toward credit, and so forth. Grants should be made first to those productive enterprises which may commence at once and which will provide goods required by the natives themselves.

The prices charged for goods distributed by the government should be set so as to discharge the obligations of the United States to the natives rather than to make a profit from operations. The cost of Administration should not be included in the mark-up of goods. Prices should be set for classes of goods rather than specifically pegged for each item. The prices of imported goods should not fluctuate widely and should be standardized with respect to quality. The sale price policy of imports should be correlated with wage levels and export sale prices so as to insure the natives purchasing power equal to that which prevailed before the war.

These elementary measures are not now in effect.[4] Their absence is a source of embarrassment to the field staffs who seek to explain existing procedures and shortages as resulting from the improvised nature of current operations. Aggressive leadership and prompt action in the provisioning of the islands with their basic necessities will contribute materially to the revitalization of the entire economy.

Notes

A. LAND

1. By 1949 most of the more obvious abuses of native land rights had been corrected.

2. By 1949 resettlement of natives on farming land had progressed considerably.

3. By 1949 administrative machinery had been set up to insure protection for native land rights, generally along the lines recommended in this Survey report.

4. This recommendation does not apply with equal relevance to all areas.

B. AGRICULTURE AND FORESTRY

1. For convenience in presenting this Summary, the several interdependent aspects of agriculture and forestry have been subdivided into "Resources" (containing background data on soils, plant distribution, plant pests and diseases, land-use planning, etc.), "Subsistence," and "Income." This section covers the first two topics; "Income" will be treated under Chapter III. This division and separation of topics which are in fact closely interrelated does some violence to continuity – with respect to agriculture, at least – but is necessitated by the over-all ordering of material in this Summary.

2. By 1949 very active measures had been undertaken to introduce effective insect control, through agency of a joint enterprise of the Navy and the Pacific Science Board of the National Research Council.

3. By 1949 the Administration had put into operation a plan for flying day-old chicks from Guam to some of the other islands.

C. FISHING

1. By 1949 there had been organized a Saipan Fishing Company, a coöperative well equipped with gear, refrigeration, and so forth.

D. HOUSING

1. By 1949 the housing situation described in this chapter had been significantly improved. Nearly all emergency camps and all mountain refuges had been replaced by more permanent types of settlement.

2. By 1949 plans had been committed to paper to operate cadastral surveys throughout the Territory, but the actual work of clearing and assigning titles still remained to be done in most cases.

E. GOODS: CONSUMER, DURABLE, PRODUCTIVE, AND CAPITAL

1. Statements about "current" (i.e., 1946) shortages require considerable revision in terms of 1949 conditions. The Naval Administration, acting through the agency of the United States Commercial Company and its successor, the Island Trading Company, has made marked progress in assuring an increasing supply of goods for the native populations. Also, many important phases of this enterprise have been turned over to individual natives and to native coöperatives.

2. These "subject" reports comprise the reports written by individual scientists for the Economic Survey; they have been recorded on microfilm and deposited in the Library of Congress.

3. Some progress has been reported in carrying out this recommendation.

4. By 1949 many of these measures had been taken, although even the Administration's most generous critic could hardly claim that all Micronesia was economically stabilized and prosperous. Many factors, some of them outside the Administration's control, contributed to a continuing shortage of some kinds of goods and services.

CHAPTER III. INCOME

A. ECONOMIC BASES

1. *General*

Prior to World War II, Micronesian natives (other than those on Guam) participated in an active island economy sponsored and directed by Japan. Natives were both direct and residual beneficiaries of the increased tempo of economic activity which Japan introduced. Natives' standards of living were affected by Japanese organization and exploitation of island resources. Natives adopted the institutional basis associated with the development. Economic benefits accruing to natives varied appreciably among islands, depending upon the type and magnitude of economic activity which was introduced by the Japanese within specific areas.

Capture of the islands and the defeat of Japan crushed the stimuli which were responsible for former economic activity in the islands. In addition, capital installations were destroyed by combat, the institutional framework upon which the previous economy rested was dislocated or discarded, and accrued benefits, such as housing, savings, and personal property, accumulated by natives over the years, were lost as casualties of war.

How can natives recover economic advantages comparable to those they had under Japanese administration? That is the problem confronting natives. The responsibility for the economic rehabilitation and recovery of natives lies primarily with the present Administration. Natives previously attained economic advantages beyond subsistence levels as a result of Japanese activity. The American Administration is responsible for providing similarly the encouragement and means for promoting native income and economic rehabilitation.

What level of native income should be the objective?

The United States Administration should establish a level of income for residents of the islands at least equal to that existing under the Japanese prior to the war. Natives lost the economic advantages of their previous income levels through no fault of their own. They wish to participate in similar benefits again. They are willing to work for them, as they did before. If the present Administration provides natives with economic means, assistance, guidance, and incentive, natives can attain economic objectives at least equal to those they previously knew.

Upon what financial basis may native rehabilitation be approached?

Natives no longer have access to their prewar savings; they have no reserves of their own on which they can draw; current income is insufficient to cover all the demands of economic rehabilitation; therefore, native rehabilitation requires outside assistance. Some aid, both in organization and support, must be supplied. The American Administration must assist in organizing the framework of finance and, like previous administrations, it must continue to provide financial assistance not only for recovery of native economic life but also for its continuation after recovery. That is one of the inescapable costs of holding the islands.

Real income of Micronesian natives is made up of two components: (1) cash income, meaning use or consumption of goods purchased with cash which, in turn, is previously derived from sale of surplus production or from wages; and (2) subsistence income, or consumption of local production which does not enter into a price economy. The relative importance of each component to total real income varies from area to area within Micronesia.

In many areas, Kapingamarangi atoll in the Carolines, for example, natives produce practically all their own food, as well as many other subsistence items. There, economic organization of native society is relatively simple, compared with many other islands or with mainland patterns. Economic organization is based primarily upon the family as a complete production and consumption unit. Money is rarely used except for exchange of goods exported to or imported from outside the normal native environment. Exchange of goods is limited. Exchanges of essentials among families are usually on a gift, obligation, or barter basis. Price considerations may be used in some exchange calculations, but institutional media for recording them are usually known only to direct participants in the transaction. In brief, biological requirements of food and numerous other subsistence needs are reasonably well satisfied with only limited marginal reliance upon money exchange and a price economy. Per capita distribution of money is extremely limited, as is also its circulation. Natives' real income in these instances comes mostly from items which do not enter a price economy, hence the magnitude of real income and the relative importance of factors entering its composition are not readily measurable. There is conclusive evidence, however, that in a number of outlying islands the total real income of natives and the accompanying standards of living are low and considerably less than in some other islands.

At the other extreme, natives of Guam, Saipan, Palau, Truk, and a number of other areas rely to a large extent upon markets, contract, money, price, and other institutional elements of a capitalist economy. There, natives produce for local subsistence, too, but they also produce for export, work for wages, offer services for sale, and in addition they rely heavily upon imports to supply essential requirements. Thus, natives' real income in such instances not only assumes greater magnitude but also the components of real income-change relationships: subsistence income decreases in relative importance while cash income increases.

No island or area depends entirely either upon subsistence income or upon cash income. Natives in the most isolated islands trade at least occasionally with outsiders. Some natives produce part of their own food and other necessities in every island, even those in which cash income assumes major importance in the native economy. Within the islands, variations apply all up and down the range between extremes in the relationship of native subsistence income and cash income. Although there are numbers of factors accounting for the variations, in general the development of cash income resources for any island has been largely a function of economic activity sponsored, either deliberately or residually, by outside sources. Metal products and other goods traded to natives provided an incentive for development of the copra trade. The sugar industry in the Marianas, and commercial fishing in other island areas, followed Japanese promotion. The presence of civilian or military personnel affected, and continues to affect, native labor requirements, services, pay rates, earning power, and purchasing power. In brief, cash income is dependent primarily upon natives' association and integration with economic systems originating outside their own islands. Also, native subsistence economy and cash income, or price economy, are inextricably intermingled in each of the islands.

Consideration of income in this and other sections of Chapter III is limited to that portion of native real income which has been labeled here as cash income. This does not mean that subsistence income and native self-sufficiency are to be ignored. It means only that techniques are not presently available for measuring the magnitude and composition of subsistence income in the native economy.

With respect to subsistence income, it is assumed that certain natives who participated only in a subsistence economy prior to the war and who still have only that are now living in approximately the same economic status as then, provided, of course, that their economic resources were not dislocated by war. Without exception, native subsistence and self-sufficiency, particularly in foodstuffs, should be encouraged.

Natives living in islands which formerly had a relatively large volume of export or import trade have had their economic status radically changed by the war. Economic casualties include not only combat damage but also economic dislocations. Comparisons of prewar and postwar income factors help to throw some light on the effects of changes in the economic status of natives.

Money circulated throughout Micronesia. A price system operated in exchange of goods within established markets. Most goods which were exported or imported between the mandated area and the Japanese home islands, as well as most goods exchanged between administrative districts within Micronesia, were handled within market institutions. Native labor was usually paid on the basis of money units. Price and wage systems have been established again by the present Administration throughout most of Micronesia.

2. *Prewar Basis for Native Income*

A brief résumé of the prewar economic situation in Micronesia may help to promote understanding of present prospects for economic development. Prior to the Japanese period economic development in Micronesia was limited almost entirely to promotion of the copra trade, the sale of small amounts of handicraft, and some development of agriculture and livestock for provisioning ships. Neither Spain nor Germany attempted a concerted colonization of the islands or intensive exploitation of the area's meager resources. During the latter part of the nineteenth century and the first decade of the twentieth, natives lived much the same as they had during the previous century. Some additional governmental services such as health and education had been introduced by the Germans, but most natives were not offered major economic opportunities differing appreciably from those they had known for generations.

The islands were brought within the economic sphere of the Japanese Empire as soon as the mandate was approved by the League of Nations. Japan analyzed the islands' resources and immediately proceeded to exploit them for a variety of reasons, such as population pressures in the home islands and a paucity of certain resources at home which outer islands might help to supplement. A colonial policy was developed by the Japanese government, and the South Seas Bureau was set up as an operating agency to carry policies into effect. Some indications of the progress of Japanese policies and development in the mandated area are offered by a comparison of immigration trends with the population of Guam, where colonization did not take place:

TABLE II. POPULATION: MANDATED MICRONESIAN ISLANDS AND GUAM

	MANDATES[a]							
	Natives							
Year	Chamorros	Kanakas[b]	Total	Japanese Nationals	Foreigners	Total Mandates	GUAM[c]	TOTAL
1920	2,824	45,681	48,505	3,671	46	52,222	13,275	65,497
1930	3,301	46,394	49,695	19,835	96	69,626	18,509	88,135
1940	4,213	46,893	51,106	84,478	124	135,708	22,290	157,998

a. Population figures for 1920 and 1930 from League of Nations Reports; for 1940 from South Seas Statistical Yearbook.

b. "Kanaka," a Polynesian term for "man," was applied by the Japanese to the indigenes of the Marshalls and Carolines. For "Chamorro," see note 3, page 9.

c. Population figures from Census of the United States.

As indicated in Table II, the Japanese population in the islands increased rapidly. The 3,671 Japanese nationals who were reported living in the islands in 1920 constituted 7.2 per cent of the total native population. By 1930, Japanese nationals had increased by 440 per cent over 1920, increasing to 19,835 persons or 28.5 per cent of the total population. By 1940 the 84,478 Japanese nationals, reported in the islands by the South Seas Statistical Yearbook, constituted 62.2 per cent of the total population. This was a 326 per cent increase in Japanese over 1930 and a 2,201 per cent increase over 1920. In 1930 there were two and one-half times as many natives as Japanese in the islands, but by 1940 there were one and three-quarters times as many Japanese as natives.

The economy of the islands changed as a result of Japanese colonization. Roads were built to open the major islands to exploitation; harbors, docks, and ways were also constructed. Land was cleared and crops were planted. Sugar cane acreage increased from 1,104 acres in 1919-20 to 11,403 acres in 1929-30, and to 30,400 acres in 1937-38. A sugar mill was built on Saipan in the early twenties; two more were built on Tinian at a later date; another was constructed on Rota in the early thirties. A distillery was built in connection with the sugar mills on Tinian; one was also built on Rota. A bag factory and also a mattress factory operated at Saipan. The Japanese developed a fishing industry on Saipan, later promoting it in a large way on Palau and Truk, with smaller installations on Ponape and in the Marshalls. Natives gathered trochus shells, trepang, and pearl shells. The Japanese home islands needed starch, so cassava production was encouraged. The home islands needed commercial fertilizers, so the Mandated Islands were prospected and additional deposits of phosphates were located. The large deposits on Angaur were systematically exploited, as also were smaller deposits on Rota, Saipan, Fais, Sonsorol, Tobi, and other islands. Bauxite was found on Babelthuap after systematic search; open-cut mining and processing plants followed.

Each of these activities involved large capital installations. In centers of primary activity demand for labor was high, as it always is in an expanding economy, and natives were employed in constructing many of the installations. Common labor found ready employment, as also did semiskilled and skilled workers. Carpenters and mechanics were at a premium. Japanese officials as well as lesser employees needed houses, and natives helped supply the demand, receiving fair rentals to support their investment. Numerous small businesses grew up to meet demands of the expanding population; most of these were in Japanese hands but natives participated to some extent, usually as wage or salaried workers rather than as individual entrepreneurs.

The timing and the direction of economic development may be indicated to some extent by a table showing distribution of Japanese colonial population.

TABLE III. DISTRIBUTION OF JAPANESE POPULATION BY DISTRICTS,[a] 1920, 1930, 1940

	1920		1930		1940	
District	Number	Per cent	Number	Per cent	Number	Per cent
Saipan	1,758	47.9	15,656	78.9	45,922	54.4
Yap	97	2.6	241	1.2	1,933	2.3
Palau	592	16.1	2,078	10.5	23,767	28.1
Truk	601	16.4	749	3.8	4,128	4.9
Ponape	425	11.6	689	3.5	8,048	9.5
Jaluit	198	5.4	422	2.1	680	.8
Total	3,671	100.0	19,835	100.0	84,478	100.0

a. Japanese administrative districts.

The Japanese first directed their attention to the Marianas. Throughout most of the twenties their major activities were centered there. This area continued to be their main center of economic activity throughout the thirties, but during this period they also began to push into other districts. Japanese emigration was accompanied by increases in trade between the mandated area and the home islands. The relative importance of trade with various islands or districts tended to accord with the movement of Japanese populations (see Table IV).

Japanese colonial policy directed emigration of nationals to islands desirable for exploitation of certain needed commodities, and economic development invariably followed the arrival of colonists. A comparison of export values from particular industries is shown in Table V.

These industries provided the basis for the economic life of the Mandated Islands. Types of economic enterprise varied among the islands as shown on Tables VI and VII. Sugar was the most important development in the Marianas. Fishing, particularly production of dried bonito, was the most important industry at Babelthuap and at Truk. Mining of phosphates was practically the only industry at Angaur and also assumed importance in Rota. Copra production continued to be the most important industry in the Marshalls.

Natives were beneficiaries of the economic enterprises which developed in their islands. They participated either directly or indirectly as laborers, suppliers, or performers of services for the new arrivals and for the enterprises which the latter brought with them.

Economic development in the islands just prior to the war may be characterized as a going concern resulting from approximately a quarter century of intensive promotion according to specific plans providing for public works, large public and private capital expenditures, high levels of employment, extensive construction, and heavy imports. Included also were services, such as education, health measures, sanitary facilities, internal security, experiment stations, and research facilities. Elements of a going economy, adjusted to a Japanese pattern, were evident in every area where the Japanese had directed attention to economic enterprise.

3. *Postwar Basis for Income*

Conquest of the islands by combat and the defeat of Japan destroyed completely the prewar economic structure. Without exception Japanese economic installations and organizations were wiped out on every island where intensive combat had taken place. Prewar sources of natives' direct or indirect income went up in smoke with them. Roads, docks, and ways remained in various states of damage and disrepair, as also did shells of some buildings.

Natives lost a quarter-century's development. They were thrown back upon resources no better, and in many respects worse, than they had when the Japanese took over. Where combat had occurred, natives lost their houses and much of their personal property. Land had been taken from them by the Japanese and for use of the occupying forces. Airstrips and other shore installations not only occupied relatively large tracts of land but also permanently destroyed for native use some of the best farm land in the islands.

Economic rehabilitation of the natives presents a more difficult problem to the present Administration than it did to the previous Japanese administration. Prospects are unfavorable for large-scale immigration, and there is far less homeland demand for exploitation of present or potential resources. On the other hand, coconut production for copra remains a basic resource, particularly in the outer islands. Presumably it may be developed to as great a degree as under former administrations. Also, on islands severely damaged by combat, reconstruction of native homes and other essentials offers short-term prospects for native employment during the next few years, provided sufficient funds are available from native income, damage claims, or other sources. Development of other agricultural production, fishing, and native industry, even though on a smaller than prewar scale, may offer prospects for comparable or better than prewar income for

TABLE IV. TOTAL VALUE OF 1940 EXPORTS AND IMPORTS BETWEEN MANDATED ISLANDS AND JAPAN, AND RELATIVE DISTRIBUTION BY SPECIFIED AREAS

	Japanese Mandated Islands			
	Exports to Japan		Imports from Japan	
Total Value (million yen)	48.5		41.2	
Distribution by specified areas				
	Per cent		Per cent	
Saipan District		56.18		40.74
Saipan	22.87		22.90	
Tinian	31.68		14.43	
Rota	1.63		3.41	
Yap District		1.97		3.05
Palau District		23.59		29.35
Palau	11.12		28.73	
Angaur	12.47		.62	
Truk District		9.56		7.56
Ponape District		6.33		14.25
Ponape	5.91		13.68	
Kusaie	.42		.57	
Jaluit District		2.37		5.05
		100.00		100.00

Source: Adapted from the South Seas Statistical Yearbook, 1940.

TABLE V. EXPORT VALUE OF SPECIFIED CATEGORIES OF COMMODITIES SHIPPED FROM MANDATED ISLANDS TO JAPAN, 1940

Rank	Item	Value Million yen
1	Sugar	20.7
2	Minerals and miscellaneous	9.1
3	Dried bonito	8.8
4	Copra	2.1
5	Rope, cord, and twine	1.3
6	Drugs and chemicals	1.0
7	Cassava starch	.7
8	Bone, horn, shell, and hides	.6
9	Alcohol	.5
10	Metal products	.5
11	Machinery, boats, and vehicles	.5

Source: Adapted from the South Seas Statistical Yearbook, 1940.

TABLE VI. EXPORTS FROM MANDATED AREA TO JAPAN, 1940; TOTAL VALUE (IN THOUSANDS OF YEN) BY SPECIFIED COMMODITIES

	Total Mandates	Saipan	Tinian	Rota	Yap	Palau	Angaur	Truk	Ponape	Kusaie	Jaluit
Plants and animals	8.7	8						.3	.1	.3	
Cassava flour	682.3	682							.3		
Other cereals, grain, starch, seed	99.7	4	1					1	94.7		
Coffee	51	50				21					
Sugar	20626.3	6645	13981	.3							
Dried bonito	8769	1289	245		33	2460		3741	1001		
Trepang	160	3			13	56		32	56		
Alcoholic beverages	470	470									
Molasses	25		25								
Other food, drink, tobacco	1595.7	396	19	178.7	22	780		164	32	2	2
Bone, horn, hides	552	13	5			523		11			
Shells	71				21	50					
Oils, fats, wares	100.8	51	.8		1	15		30	3		
Drugs and chemicals	1057	311	697			28			21		
Rope, cordage, twine	1320	33	8		53	112		83	826	87	118
Paints, dyes, cosmetics	17.9	13	4			.9					
Coconut fiber	306					2		66	126		112
Cloth	91	27	10		2	33		4	11		4
Clothing and ornaments	57	16	12			24		2	3		
Pulp, paper, books	3.3	1	.5			.9		.5			.4
Pottery and glass	108.3	12	10		.4	56		10	19		.9
Metal products	494.2	187	59		30	85		46	65	.2	22
Machinery, boats, vehicles	478	122	113		7	85		64	60	3	24
Copra	2140	128			247	123		270	378	82	912
Charcoal	5.4		3			1		.4		1	
Miscellaneous products	9187.6	559	74	606	523	902	6011	144.6	282	29	57
Total	48477.2										

Source: Adapted from the South Seas Statistical Yearbook, 1940.

TABLE VII. IMPORTS FROM JAPAN TO MANDATED AREA, 1940; TOTAL VALUE (IN THOUSANDS OF YEN) BY SPECIFIED COMMODITIES

	Total Mandates	Saipan	Tinian	Rota	Yap	Palau	Angaur	Truk	Ponape	Kusaie	Jaluit
Plants and animals	238.9	8	.8	209	.9	6		.2	14		
Cereals, grain, starch, seed	5478	1389	950	202	160	1289	26	449	772	14	227
Rice	4853	1264	858	183	140	1129	22	400	666	9	192
Flour	178.3	16	30	4	15	36	.3	11	31	3	32
Food, drink, tobacco	7034	1344	760	205	270	1958	68	623	1095	58	653
Soya sauce	313	54	45	11	8	122	5	19	41	1	7
Soy-bean paste	354	101	54	9	12	91	2	32	45	2	6
Sugar	20.1	4	2	.4	.1	6	1	2	4	.6	
Candy	515	53	25	13	21	127	4	49	99	13	111
Vegetables	373	71	34	7	10	103	3	27	91	3	24
Canned goods	806	48	60	9	60	201	14	80	150	19	165
Cider, citron	113.9	14	8	.1	4	24	1	24	27	.8	11
Refined sake	169	25	11	4	6	56	.7	26	21	1	18
Beer	958	162	107	47	31	343	3	65	161	2	37
Bone, shell, horn	84.9	10	18	1	5	31	.5	7	12	.4	
Oils, fats, waxes	2696	772	249	87	45	720	6	235	402	25	155
Drugs and chemicals	1681	328	182	66	57	646	12	97	207	6	80
Paint, dyes, cosmetics	353.3	78	31	15	5	128	.3	45	28	2	21
Rope, cordage, thread	512	93	50	12	13	172	16	36	76	4	40
Cloth	3618	940	994	91	102	550	14	274	354	23	276
Cotton	858	229	110	25	43	158	3	93	97	4	96
Linen	1522	366	813	2	38	32		67	84	14	106
Clothing and ornaments	2555	569	279	107	95	675	10	217	436	27	140
Pulp, paper, books	852	206	89	20	32	290	2	46	100	4	63
Minerals	937	159	434	17	12	205	4	36	54	5	11
Pottery and glass	573	97	64	15	16	166	2	31	143	4	35
Metal products	2568	508	288	83	64	796	24	163	551	16	75
Machinery parts for vehicles, boats, watches	5100	913	780	97	141	2025	32	379	598	18	117
Miscellaneous	7021	1976	746	169	237	2423	39	461	768	27	175
Lumber	2394.9	561	204	25	126	1011	15	204	209	.9	39
Total	41202										

Source: Adapted from the South Seas Statistical Yearbook, 1940.

natives if ownership and control, with consequent benefits, are shifted to natives. Such a policy might be applied gradually, for the assumption of ownership and control will involve risks as well as benefits. Aid and direction should be extended to help natives establish business connections with outside interests and to help reduce risks, while maintaining the main objective of improving income not only through promotion of desirable and feasible activities but also through participation of natives in the islands' economic activity. Some services are already being provided. Improvements and extensions may reasonably be anticipated. Construction of public facilities, such as schools, dispensaries, hospitals, and government buildings will create a demand for labor. Medical facilities may be shifted gradually to native hands as medical practitioners and nurses are trained. Already most teachers are natives. Although their educational background may leave much to be desired, training programs may be instituted which will help to qualify them for their important responsibilities. Special efforts should be directed to locating skills and talents among natives which will allow them to take over more and more public services which were previously supplied by the Japanese and which, otherwise, must be supported by American personnel. Relative freedom of movement among islands is desirable if natives are to be allowed full opportunity to accept voluntary employment where demands for labor exist. The framework of a new economy must be built up on native resources, including land and labor, with capital derived from non-native sources.

Natives now earn some income from labor, from manufacture of copra and handicraft, from operation of small fishing enterprises, and from some trading enterprises. Income from these sources could and should be expanded and supplemented by development of new sources. The following sections in Chapter III describe these income-producing activities in some detail. They should be read with the understanding that conditions do and will continue to vary from island to island. Guam's income problems are entirely different from those of, say, Palau or even Saipan. Guamians' wage employment opportunities are far more numerous because of the naval base there. Truk will have to depend less on wage income and more on manufacture of copra and handicraft, as will the Marshalls. Fishing may develop into a major income source at Palau, if properly planned and organized.

The important thing is that the Administration begin immediately the preparation of a blueprint for economic rehabilitation to cover the specific needs and conditions of each area, and proceed vigorously to carry out the program. Unforeseen factors will undoubtedly crop up and dictate changes in the program, but those in no way minimize the value of a comprehensive program.

B. INCOME LEVELS

Members of the Editorial Board recommend a restoration of natives' prewar level of income as an immediate objective for economic planning in Micronesia. American attitudes of fair play and equity dictate that these people should fare at least as well with us as under our former enemies; our newly acquired wards naturally will not be satisfied with less.

Prior to the war natives' incomes were not high according to American standards, but they were quite good for that part of the world and, for the area as a whole, considerably higher than at present. Mandate islanders earned incomes under the Japanese, particularly during the thirties, that were much higher than they had been under either the Germans or the Spanish. Also, natives' average incomes were favorable when compared with those of native residents in islands to the west and much better than natives' incomes in many islands to the south. The mandated area's expanding economy, as described in the previous section, offered opportunities to natives for acquiring favorable incomes through their labor or property. There, wage rates and producers' prices were lower than in America; so were prices of Japanese goods which natives bought. Natives could and did purchase a variety of goods in substantial quantities. Today, as compared with the prewar period, natives' incomes are considerably less, quantities and varieties of imported goods are also less, and costs of goods are higher.

The extent to which natives' present incomes fall short of previous levels may be indicated in several ways. During the Survey, representative samples of natives' incomes were taken in several areas. On Yap a fourth of the families with incomes in 1939 now have none. Among those with current incomes, the average amount received each month dropped from $25.99[1] in 1939 to $15.98 in 1946. Residents of Palau experienced even greater declines in income. In 1939 the average Palau family had a monthly income of $44.33; the same group's average monthly income in 1946 was $14.57. On Rota there were only 31.5 per cent as many wage earners in 1946 as there were in 1940, and the average monthly earnings dropped from $14.22 to $11.54. In addition, in each area individual savings were frozen and unavailable, homes were destroyed, and personal property was largely dissipated.

Concurrently with losses in income, purchasing power of specific income units also declined. An analysis of prewar costs of selected commodities in terms of earning capacity compared with costs and earning capacity indicates that natives must now work longer – when work is available, which is not commonly the case – to purchase the same goods. A cost-of-living "basket" of these selected commodities would have cost islanders 93.9 per cent more on the basis of United States wholesale prices for August 1946 than the same commodities cost on the average during 1936-1940 in the Tokyo wholesale market. Thus, natives were squeezed by both edges of the vise – losses in cash income and rising costs of goods.

Dissatisfaction among natives is inescapable in this situation which was created through no fault of their own. Islanders look to the present Administration, as they did to previous administrations, for aid in working out their economic destiny.

An approach to restoration of natives' prewar levels of income involves consideration of a complex of factors, chief among which are wage rates and volume of employment; producers' prices and volume of products for sale; variety and volume of imported goods, and prices which natives have to pay for them. Prewar levels of income may be approached in one or more of several ways: either wages may be raised and more work opportunities provided; or prices for native products and volume of native production may be increased; or costs of goods may be lowered, along with increases in the variety and volume of goods available for sale. Administrative action will be required in each case.

The Editorial Board urges that all these interrelated approaches should be utilized, immediately and concurrently. Adjustments must be made, particularly upward adjustments in the income-producing factors.

There is no danger of inflation from such administrative actions. As long as goods are available, natives will concentrate on purchasing their necessities, which will absorb all their purchasing power. They previously had many more goods than now; natives need them again; they want the chance to buy them. Additional income, with a greater volume and variety of goods, will make possible a restoration of prewar levels of living rather than lead to "runaway" prices. Trade-store prices are controlled. There is no evidence of secondary markets among natives. Group controls are strong among natives and any tendency to engage in transactions outside established channels is unpopular. Hence, the inflation factor is not a serious force operating in the economy and should not be used to determine wage rates and price levels for native produce.

Native wage rates should be raised. An individual's earnings for given units of labor, such as a day's or a week's work, should allow him to purchase at least as much goods as he could for a similar amount and kind of work prior to the war. A number of native workers are now employed in other than their chosen skill or craft. They should be reclassified and paid in accordance with the skill they apply to their job. Opportunities for work should be broadened by initiation of public works and other Administration-sponsored rehabilitation projects. A corollary, although somewhat longer-term, objective should be: like wages for like work, whether it be in Hawaii, Guam, or Ponape. Perhaps the corollary policy cannot be put in effect in one move or even in ten moves, but it is nevertheless a sound and equitable objective. The other considerations – wage rates and additional opportunities for jobs – are pressing. They deserve administrative action immediately.[2]

Prices for products natives sell should be raised in every possible instance, not only to increase income but also to stimulate maximum production. Native producers, like all other producers, want the best prices they can get. They are entitled, like other producers, to sell to their best advantage. Natives have virtually no opportunity as yet for selling in market outlets in other than those provided by the Administration. The Administration, owing to the monopoly position it has been forced to assume in the Micronesian market, has assumed also the direct responsibility of promoting efficient and inexpensive marketing. For natives, as well as for other producers, this means in practical operation the best prices the current market offers in the most favorable markets with only minimum deductions for marketing costs. To the Administration, it means investigation of market outlets for island produce with the objective of making best possible sales and the elimination of all unnecessary costs.[3]

Native income from local production depends not only upon prices received but also upon volume of production. Greater production is not only badly needed but also entirely possible. Increased prices will help in some measure to stimulate production; however, more producers' goods and restored or newly installed production facilities are also necessary for natives to expand production. These goods and facilities must be made available, by outright grant if necessary, to increase native self-support. None too incidentally, the sooner natives are in a position to contribute substantially to their own self-support, the sooner the Federal Treasury will be relieved of high administrative expenses.

The sales' cost of some goods should be lowered. Distribution costs on all goods should always be held to a minimum upon the accepted theory that present operating agencies are in the area primarily to serve the native population rather than to profit from them. Pricing policies for various categories of goods are developed in a later section, "Finance"; in brief they are as follows: Consumers' goods, i.e., those items purchased daily, should be priced on the basis of cost at outgoing port plus distribution; producers' goods, i.e., items such as tools, livestock, etc., which enable natives to increase their production, should be based upon costs at outgoing ports plus or minus margins which bring the final price to natives into line with prewar costs and income relationships; capital goods, i.e., machinery, shore installations, construction materials, etc., should be priced below replacement costs and sold to natives often at virtually nominal prices. In addition, natives' needs in some instances constitute emergency situations, and the Administration should step in and provide natives with such goods, particularly those required for production, regardless of their present ability to pay.

C. UNPAID CLAIMS

The Administration charged with economic rehabilitation of Micronesia must not overlook any measure which can contribute to the general objective. Measures like development of valuable natural resources along with utilization of native skills will undoubtedly be undertaken: they are so obvious. Less obvious but almost as important is the native "resource" of unpaid claims.

For decades Micronesians have been investing their energies and their resources in building up capital goods and production goods and financial reserves, both for livelihood and for economic security. Then the war – for which they were not responsible and in which they hardly participated except as victims – brought about mass destruction of most of their goods and reserves. Assuming that the Administration will in any case have to finance recovery, the problem arises: Should the Administration support this economic revolution, this leveling of economic status, by ignoring past achievements, or should it undertake to restore the lost investments? The Board favors the second alternative for two main reasons: (1) It is more in line with American political and economic concepts of equity; and (2) it will provide one additional source of assistance for the complex task of rehabilitating the native economy.

Measures are already being undertaken to recover war losses for the Guamians: a commission is at work compiling claims, and equitable adjustments are anticipated. Not so fortunate are the natives living on Saipan and Rota, or the Marshallese and Carolinians. These former wards of the League of Nations are not "nationals" or "citizens" of Japan; they are "residents" of the islands, and as such are "foreigners" to the United States. There is no precedent for presentation and recovery of claims under such circumstances.[1] Nor at present do these political dependents possess any representation through which they can secure equity or even sympathetic hearing for their claims. But under State Department ruling and Public Law 39 of the 78th United States Congress, these natives are *entitled* to compensation for certain of their losses. Their claims include:

1. Claims against Japan for losses sustained as a result of actions which violated the League mandate. Under this heading would fall Japanese seizures of property, and so forth, before and during the war, and all war (combat) damages; Japan violated League mandate by waging aggressive warfare.
2. Claims against the United States for war losses sustained as a result of United States actions committed in violation of the laws of war.
3. Claims against the United States for losses sustained as a result of United States actions after the time of securing of the areas.

With respect to (1), it is the recommendation of this Board that the Administration immediately set out to adjust such claims and later seek to reimburse itself from reparations, acting as agent for the natives who would otherwise remain unrepresented. Peace-treaty making will move slowly and reparations will not materialize for years, if ever. The United States government can afford better than can its Micronesian wards to wait to collect the relatively small sums involved, which to the Micronesians are not at all small.

With respect to (2) and (3), it is recommended that the claims commission institution be extended throughout Micronesia for the purpose of hearing and establishing claims against the United States government. It should not be difficult to define losses sustained by natives as a result of the direct requisition, on the part of our forces, of land and facilities for military or other purposes. Natives can be counted upon to itemize accurately and in great detail all such losses they have sustained or that they continue to sustain (that is, native lands now being held for military camps, airstrips, and so forth).

Less clear but just as important are questions concerning native funds and savings deposits. When Military Government officials established jurisdiction over natives in the Mandated Islands, they exchanged yen currency of natives at the rate of twenty yen to a dollar and to a limit of fifty dollars a native. Yet surpluses above that exchanged for dollars were collected and individual owners given receipts. Military Government now holds this yen currency along with other "captured documents," with no apparent plan for restoration.

At the time, the measure of limiting exchange was justified: Military Government did not have sufficient funds to effect a total exchange, and, furthermore, larger numbers of dollars in native hands *at that time* may have increased inflationary pressures brought about through the scarcity of goods available for purchase. On the other hand, the establishment of an exchange rate of twenty to one cannot be justified.

This Board recommends that the prewar exchange rate of approximately four yen to a dollar be reëstablished for Micronesia, and that this be extended retroactively to the dates of occupation to permit an adjustment of natives' yen already exchanged for dollars.

And further, it is recommended that non-exchanged yen which were taken up and receipted for by Military Government be returned to individual and community owners in dollars, as soon as the possibility of inflation is removed by the appearance of more goods in the area.

Natives' postal savings merit special attention. Many natives saved part of their prewar cash income by accumulating it as yen currency, postal savings, or bank deposits (in the few places where banks operated). Some natives cached currency; others, acting prudently they thought, deposited their currency with the Japanese postal-savings system. Those natives who held currency until the arrival of United States occupying forces were directed to exchange it for dollars or for Military Government receipts. Thereby, these natives already have at least partial dollar reimbursement for their currency savings and a written promise by an authorized Federal agency for ultimate redemption of the balance. Others, or perhaps part of the same group, who previously deposited yen with the postal-savings system, have only Japanese receipts as their evidence of assets. These receipts, at one time, were as good as yen currency; they had the same backing. Natives looked upon the postal receipts as valuable assets, just as important to them as similar evidence of hard earnings are to us. They now need, and they could use to great advantage, the cash equivalent of these savings.

Natives in Palau verified postal-savings claims amounting to 687,500 yen. Rota natives have postal savings listed to the sum of 10,163 yen, and, in addition, Chamorros have a community claim of slightly more than 11,000 yen for a savings deposit in the Bank of Saipan. Saipan natives also deposited savings with the postal-savings system as well as with the Bank of Saipan. Military Government officials were directed after occupation to obtain records of postal savings of natives. Presumably these records are available. If not, new records of postal savings can be developed easily with native assistance, for they can readily produce ample evidence to prove up individual claims.

Liquidation of claims including receipts for yen currency (at the equitable exchange rate), for postal savings, and for claims against banks, would help to provide natives with badly needed purchasing and investment power and would also go far in establishing natives' confidence in the present Administration. It is assumed that the Administration will attempt to reimburse itself for these expenditures, or rather for these "advances of funds," out of reparations, for clearly many of these items represent justified claims against Japan. Natives, however, cannot afford to wait for the ultimate settling of their claims in international parleys. They need the money now and, if they can get it now, the Administration will not be required to spend as much on subsidizing other methods of rehabilitation.[1]

D. LABOR

It is essential that the native workers in Micronesia be employed gainfully in productive enterprises. These should provide to all who are able to work the chance either to earn sufficient income or to produce sufficient goods to support their families at the levels which prevailed before the war. It is the obligation of the Administration to distribute the employment opportunities so that work is available as far as possible to every section of the population.

The prevalent notion concerning the labor supply in Micronesia is that it is cheap, abundant, and expendable. From the standpoint of native welfare, however, *manpower must be considered as one of the most valuable assets, limited in amount and requiring discriminating utilization.* Productive output per man is lower than in the United States because of less mechanization, climatic conditions, the physical condition of the population, and native social customs. Labor, therefore, should be treated as a valuable resource along with other resources of the area. Another mistaken viewpoint is that native labor is unskilled and of coolie quality. There are many highly skilled workers in Micronesia. The total output could be increased greatly by the allocation of natives to employments which utilize their specialized skills and by managing them with due regard to their actual social characteristics.

Major efforts should be directed toward increasing the percentage of the population able to work and toward heightening the productivity of laborers. This includes the following: (1) increased medical care for the sick and injured so that involuntary idleness due to these causes can be kept at a minimum; (2) careful selection of work projects which benefit the islands and their occupants, not "made-work" jobs; (3) the screening of manpower to determine the existing occupational aptitudes and their use in activities where they can be most productive; (4) provision of technical training to unskilled workers to increase their effectiveness; (5) the development of incentives for work; and (6) the introduction of equipment and tools which would enhance productivity. How some of these requirements may be accomplished is discussed below.

Americans should not judge native work standards by their own work habits. One of the most important factors in motivating the native worker is the kind of personal relationship existing between the supervisor and the worker. The islander identifies his interest more with the man who supervises the job than with the employment itself. Absenteeism from work has been directly traced to frequent changes in overseers, and low productivity to poor personal relationships between the supervisors and the workers. Because the supervisor is so critical a factor, the Administration should exercise more care in the choice of personnel for the assignments. Supervisors should have enough technical knowledge of the project underway as well as sufficient understanding of the natives to command the respect of the worker. Beyond this, the motivations for work vary as much as the native cultures themselves. In Palau, competition between traditional work groups will step up the output sharply, whereas in Yap this can occur only through appeals for coöperative efforts. Contrasts in work incentives are in evidence in divergent native attitudes toward income. In Yap, the native workers will labor energetically when they see desired goods for immediate purchase at the local store, whereas in Palau the workers visualize the advantages of earning money for future expenditures and, therefore, will accept employment even when there is no imminent prospect of utilizing the income. Within a single culture, there are equally significant variations in work appeals. The Japanese learned that in the bauxite-mining industry of Palau, the option of piece work with liberal bonuses for extra output or a flat daily wage appealed to two different types of workers. The introduction of the two systems resulted in a decisive increase in the total output of both groups. These are but a few illustrations of the kinds of questions which should be considered in the administration of labor in each area. In general, it is sound policy to discover and use the incentives already meaningful to the workers rather than to attempt to introduce a distinctly new set. Every native society has some schemes for inducing individuals to produce; the labor officer should concentrate on developing a positive set of rewards in line with local customs.

Labor should be entirely voluntary. The volition must be more than a nominal one. No one should be *forced* to work by direct or indirect methods. No penalties should be levied against anyone refusing to accept a particular kind of employment. There is little danger that the natives would prefer total idleness to work; if the proper opportunities and conditions prevail, every native will be productive in some activity.

Workers violating work regulations should be subject only to penalties posted in advance. The determination of the disciplining of workers should be in consultation with the native chiefs and native magistrates. Disciplinary measures will vary from one area to another; the same actions will not be effective in all social groups. Violations should be immediately called to the attention of the individual concerned and his chief, and penalties administered in a consistent manner. The penalties must not include the administration of any form of bodily injury, the banishment of a worker and his family to another island, or the punishment of the native chief for the acts of one of his people. These penalties occasionally have been used and have provoked resentment rather than

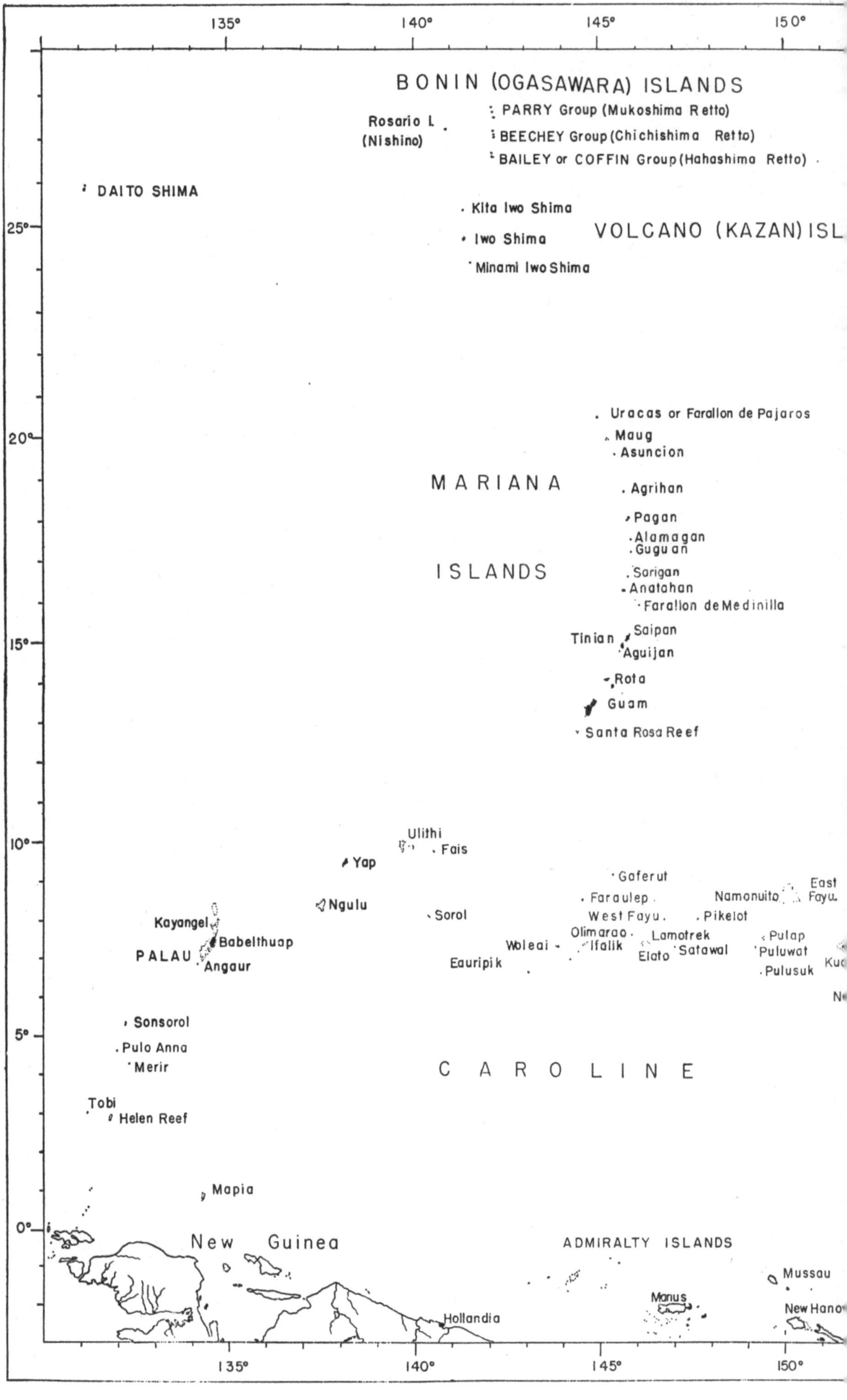

135°
140°
145°
150°
BONIN (OGASAWARA) ISLANDS
PARRY Group (Mukoshima Retto)
BEECHEY Group (Chichishima Retto)
BAILEY or COFFIN Group (Hahashima Retto)
Rosario I. (Nishino)
DAITO SHIMA
Kita Iwo Shima
Iwo Shima
Minami Iwo Shima
VOLCANO (KAZAN) ISL
25°
20°
15°
10°
5°
0°
Uracas or Farallon de Pajaros
Maug
Asuncion
MARIANA
ISLANDS
Agrihan
Pagan
Alamagan
Guguan
Sarigan
Anatahan
Farallon de Medinilla
Saipan
Tinian
Aguijan
Rota
Guam
Santa Rosa Reef
Ulithi
Fais
Yap
Ngulu
Sorol
Gaferut
Faraulep
West Fayu
Namonuito
East Fayu
Pikelot
Olimarao
Lamotrek
Ifalik
Satawal
Elato
Woleai
Eauripik
Pulap
Puluwat
Pulusuk
Kayangel
Babelthuap
PALAU
Angaur
Sonsorol
Pulo Anna
Merir
Tobi
Helen Reef
CAROLINE
Mapia
New Guinea
ADMIRALTY ISLANDS
Mussau
Manus
New Hano
Hollandia

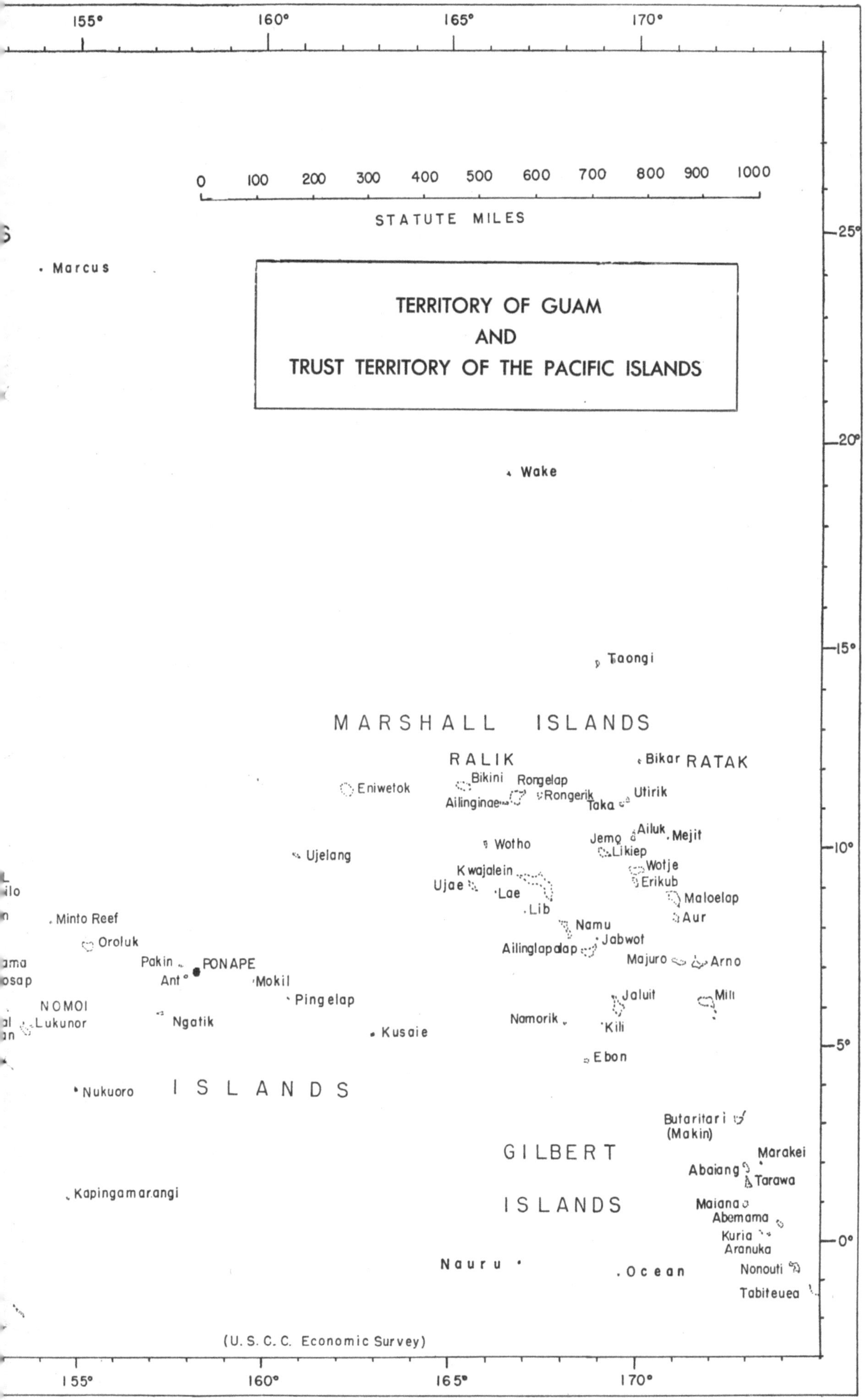
155°
160°
165°
170°
0
100
200
300
400
500
600
700
800
900
1000
STATUTE MILES
25°
20°
15°
10°
5°
0°
TERRITORY OF GUAM
AND
TRUST TERRITORY OF THE PACIFIC ISLANDS
Marcus
Wake
Taongi
MARSHALL ISLANDS
RALIK
RATAK
Bikar
Eniwetok
Bikini
Rongelap
Ailinginae
Rongerik
Taka
Utirik
Ailuk
Mejit
Jemo
Likiep
Wotho
Ujelang
Wotje
Erikub
Kwajalein
Ujae
Lae
Lib
Maloelap
Aur
Namu
Jabwot
Ailinglapalap
Majuro
Arno
Minto Reef
Oroluk
Pakin
PONAPE
Ant
Mokil
Pingelap
NOMOI
Lukunor
Ngatik
Kusaie
Jaluit
Mili
Namorik
Kili
Ebon
Nukuoro
ISLANDS
Butaritari
(Makin)
GILBERT
ISLANDS
Marakei
Abaiang
Tarawa
Maiana
Abemama
Kuria
Aranuka
Kapingamarangi
Nauru
Ocean
Nonouti
Tabiteuea
(U. S. C. C. Economic Survey)

achievement of discipline. It has been amply demonstrated in Micronesia that an adequate system of rewards, understanding supervisors, and respect for native customs preclude the need for discipline with but rare exceptions.

Laborers should have the right to appeal their grievances to appropriate authority and, if necessary, to the highest authority. Individual natives exercising this prerogative should not be penalized but viewed as engaged in the legitimate and normal economic negotiations between employer and employee. Natives tend to act in concert in dealing with their employers. They use their chiefs as spokesmen. Such actions are in keeping with native traditions and should not be interpreted as being unauthorized and subject to punishment.

The amount of rehabilitation to be accomplished in islands devastated by war is so great that there is no need for workers to be employed away from their home islands. Laborers should be used as far as possible in their home villages. Only where no local opportunities exist should natives be offered the chance to work on another island. If employed off their home islands, a formal contract should be prepared giving the conditions of employment in detail and restricting the period away from home to six months. Government has as much obligation to fulfill the provisions of the contract as has any other group. No worker should be taken from those areas which are suffering from a depleted population or from a local shortage of manpower. Work projects should be reoriented so that workers can live with their families at home while employed. The present practice of having laborers live away from home near work projects is demoralizing family and community life.

Public works should be devised so that laborers will be employed on projects of direct benefit to the natives. Only after this type of work has been taken care of fully – and this will require many years – should the military forces employ native labor in support of military activities. A higher priority should be maintained for essential native rehabilitation projects, such as the rebuilding of homes, villages, and canoes, the replanting of farms and trees, the cultivation of crops, and the reconstruction of basic public utilities, than for other types of installations or for the serving of military personnel. This principle has been issued as a directive but is as yet to be implemented in the field. Laborers on Saipan are used so heavily in the operation of military activities that they are unable to undertake their own rehabilitation. Yap natives have not had a chance to rebuild their homes. Peleliu workers are unable to redevelop their food resources. These are but a few instances of a common practice on the part of the Administration.[1]

The labor market should be coördinated. The employment officer should compile and maintain an active list of employables and their skills. The locally unemployed should be given preference over foreign labor if they can fulfill the qualifications for the job. The practice on Angaur of importing unskilled Japanese laborers despite the presence of a large labor pool of idle native workmen in Palau should be abandoned. The utilization of labor should take into account the needs of the entire population for gainful employment. In Truk and Palau laborers are hired because of the convenience of their location rather than with regard to the need for work. As a result, one district has a high rate of employment and others, equally needy, have none. If jobs are few in number they should be allocated so that all groups have equal opportunities for work.

Casual, mass-labor recruitment should give way to orderly procedures involving the selection of individual workers based on aptitude and their assignment to types of work which can make greater use of their skills. At present, carpenters, machinists, and mechanics are used as common laborers on road repair and no one knows who the skilled craftsmen are or what they are doing. The younger generation of men need vocational guidance. Many of the workers are eager to learn useful trades: a training-on-the-job program could be developed along with a vocational education program in the school system. The policy should be to open the channels of advancement so that qualified natives can become eligible for any position. This policy should be implemented by assisting and encouraging natives to prepare for these appointments. The ultimate objectives of such a program would be the extension of native responsibility over their own economic life.

In the management of labor, native work customs should be respected. The traditional division of labor between men and women, older and younger persons, as well as between different social classes, should be used in the grouping of workers and the selection of native labor bosses. Members of one ethnic group should not be placed in charge of another whenever it is apt to lead to dissension. No attempt should be made to reform native society through the manipulation of the labor market. Workers should not be expected to violate their social customs in order to comply with the job regulations. This has occurred on Angaur and has resulted in deep resentment among the natives.

All workers should be *paid* for work performed for the Administration or other sections of the armed forces. Pay should be calculated in terms of money. In those areas where workers are unable to provide their own subsistence while on the job, arrangements should be made for them to procure it at a reasonable cost which may be deducted from their wages. Local customs should be considered in determining this matter.

The existing differentials in wage scales among the islands are due to historic accident. These differences should be eliminated as soon as feasible. It will take time to equate all of the islands, but there are no insurmountable barriers to the achievement of this practice. The only permanent basis of differences in wages which should be used is that of the technical skill of the work performed. To facilitate the development of a wage system based on skill of work performed, the wage boards already ordered to be set up for the entire area should in fact be placed in operation. These boards should develop a classification system which would establish wage rates based on skill required for the performance of the task. The present categories, skilled and unskilled, can be replaced by a more realistic and detailed job-analysis schedule. The payment of chiefs reveals the lack of a systematic wage schedule. In some areas they are not paid any wage, while their assistants are. In Truk, all chiefs are paid an identical wage regardless of whether they are in charge of less than a hundred or more than several thousand natives. In this, and other instances, a standardized scale was used by the Japanese and could be developed by a wage board once again. These boards should meet at regular intervals to review prior decisions, examine inequities, and relate wage levels to purchasing power.

The minimum wages should be sufficient to provide for every full-time worker enough purchasing power to secure a level of living at least equal to that which prevailed before the war. This condition does not prevail today. The discrepancy between wages and prices is so great that the average gainfully employed person on many islands has a submarginal standard of living. Wage scales should be geared to allow individuals in each of the income brackets to approach their prewar standards of living.

The present wage rate is interpreted as *the* wage; it should be interpreted as the minimum. The established minimum wages should not be construed as prohibiting the payment of higher wages by private enterprises which employ natives. The present wage schedule is now interpreted as the maximum allowable wages on Angaur.

The schedule of hours and days of work should be reëxamined by the proposed wage board. During the war period it was necessary to use native workers at the times most suitable to the armed forces. The native economy, the climate, and native work habits do not fit into the American work schedule. The designated hours should allow the natives an opportunity to care for their subsistence needs and to engage in work when weather conditions are more conducive to intensive labor. In establishing the hours and days of work, the emphasis should be on employment during the periods when the maximum output can be secured rather than on continuous physical presence on the job. Natives traditionally work hard for certain intervals of time, but hard work for long hours day after day is not the rule. It would be more effective to assign definite work tasks that can be finished in four or five hours than to keep a man at work for eight hours just because we are accustomed to this period of daily work. The existing, prolonged work schedule causes native workers to withdraw suddenly from the job, leaving the project supervisor indignant over the alleged irresponsibility of the natives. Total output would increase with a more realistic time schedule and would enable the natives to integrate their paid employment with their subsistence activities.

Workmen's compensation should be provided to protect natives against permanent and temporary disabilities from injuries occurring while employed. Workers should be insured against permanent disability. Natives temporarily invalided as a result of work accidents should be retained on the payroll at their regular wage rate until deemed able to work again by the medical officer. Safety measures should be adopted. Native operators of motor vehicles should be required to pass a driving test and thereafter licensed. Users of dangerous machinery should be given ample instructions and be provided with adequate protective devices. Many of the serious accidents which have occurred were due to lack of these elementary precautions.

The present restrictions on the employment of children should be maintained.

Private contractors employing natives should deal in all cases through the Administration. The type of control over natives now exercised by the contractor on Angaur should not be permitted. Formal contracts should be made which stipulate the wages and hours of work, conditions and provisions, and so forth. It is the responsibility of the Administration to insure the enforcement of contracts. Contractors failing to abide by the regulations should be subject to fixed penalties and other forms of discipline.

The effectiveness of native labor could be improved through the provision of adequate tools. Some Micronesians are highly skilled in the use of small machines, and efforts may well be directed toward the securing of equipment which would allow them to make many of their necessities. The tools and equipment required by the economy should be the subject of a special study. While some military materials are usable, especially in the immediate period, it would be unwise to assume that these supplies are adequate for present or future native needs. Army and Navy war vehicles are too costly to operate and too difficult to replace. They were designed for combat for short periods and not for prolonged use. Machinery produced for the American market, too, has specialized features which are not entirely suitable to Micronesia. The islands require machinery which will withstand weathering, operate at low speeds, and involve small rather than large work groups. There is need for specialized tools. The natives have work habits that are as fixed as those of any skilled trade in the United States. Makeshift tools greatly limit effective work today. Hence, it is recommended that a mechanical expert be called upon to explore the technological requirements of the natives and the manufacturers capable of producing the needed items at a reasonable cost.

A labor policy which meets the practical needs of the islands will make not only for greater production, efficiency in use of manpower, and a coöperative population, but also for a balanced economy. The center of the problem is good management.[2]

E. AGRICULTURE AND FORESTRY

1. *Copra*

Copra has been in the past, and represents for the future, the principal cash crop available to the native. Total annual Micronesian production in years before the war reached an estimated 15,000 tons.

During the war shipment was impossible; what copra was on hand when shipping was discontinued molded and spoiled and was not salable when it could be moved. As a result, and because labor was needed for other purposes, the production ceased. With authority passing to the Americans in 1944, an effort was made to revive the industry, both to provide a source of income for the islanders and to produce a vegetable fat which is in scarce supply. Production began slowly and during 1945 the Marshall Islands produced approximately 109 tons, paying the native at the rate of $40 per long ton for the best grade. This amount of production is far short of the reputed Japanese receipts for 1938 of 6380 short tons.

There are numerous factors entering into the production and purchase of copra which should properly be the subject of a comprehensive study in itself.

The prevailing price of $40 per long ton set by the Administration was based on data from wage rates, time required, and prevailing costs of trade goods. Because the circumstances were unfavorable, owing to uncertain shipping facilities for picking up the copra, the lack of sufficient and suitable knives, the employment of the natives as workers on military projects and other causes, the production lagged, the volume remained low, and the price did not greatly improve.[1]

Copra production is a variable industry in Micronesia. In the Marshall Islands it can be prepared with sun drying and the product is usually of comparatively high grade. The equipment is simple, the quantities are small, and, unless prepared in a period of weather marked by rain and high humidity, the copra is of excellent quality. In the islands where rain is more prevalent, some simple arrangements are made for heat drying, which results in a poorer product, depreciated in appearance owing to smoke, probably delayed drying, and being kept under humid conditions which encourage molds and some spoilage. The majority of the islands are not now in production at all. On some the natives claim that the effects of war have destroyed numbers of trees, so that the remainder is required for subsistence. On others there has been some justifiable complaint that the workers were absent in large numbers. In one place there is dispute concerning the division of income between the laborers and the plantation owner or chiefs; elsewhere there is an acute shortage of knives. It is believed that if the price paid to the natives would materially increase, production would be stimulated in a very considerable way.

The natives of Micronesia are under some disadvantage in the production of copra compared with producers in the Philippines, the Netherland Indies, and other large copra centers of the tropical world. The Germans organized the islands to a considerable degree, increased planting, laid out paths, and taught the natives the techniques of production. In many cases the tree yield of nuts is low, and in most cases the strain of tree produces nuts which are small. It appears that there is a variation from 3500 to more than 5000 nuts in the number required to produce a ton of copra, and that in the Micronesian area generally the higher quantities are necessary. There is also a difference in the efficiency with which the work is accomplished; one study made elsewhere shows that estate management is at a much higher level of production than native management, sometimes as much as 100 per cent increased production resulting from expert management alone. This would be accounted for in plantation practice regarding care of groves, health of trees, use of all available nuts, prevention of spoilage, and no loss of nuts through waste and neglect. Native management prevails in the islands generally, with what efficiency it is not now known.

At the moment of writing the outlook for copra is good. However, the Philippines have been able to go into production almost on the scale attained before the war and may surpass it for the fiscal year. The plantations there have not been greatly damaged, and there is abundant labor. The price has risen greatly, and the market seems to be able to absorb all that can be offered. The American market will not pay an appreciable premium for good quality, since practically all of the pressed coconut oil goes into soapmaking. By contrast, the European market requires and uses a large amount for edible fats. The Philippines' smoke-dried copra will receive practically the same price in the American market that the sun-dried Micronesian product receives. If there is a small percentage of fatty acid in the oil, it is not a factor in soapmaking, as it is with edible oils.

The concern of the Survey is with both native and plantation operation, replanting of devastated areas, and supplying of materials needed for drying, such as wire screen, tin roofing and accessories, bags for shipping, and above all proper knives. The labor which is required for full-scale production is still lacking. The producers in the Marshalls, mostly working as families, turn out small quantities, usually less than a ton per collection, and have still to do much to restore their plantings to full capacity. The operations in the larger islands, such as Ponape, Kusaie, and Guam, are generally on the plantation scale. Some of the plantations have fallen into inevitable neglect and have become overgrown with shrubs and vines, for which considerable labor is needed to put them into operating condition. It is believed that good production would be at the rate of a ton per man per month.

The coconut palms in production in Micronesia are principally of the small nut strain. In a replanting scheme strict attention should be paid to size of nuts, history of the strain for production per tree, resistance to disease if any, and acclimatization. The promiscuous selection of nuts for planting should be discouraged. The preferred distance for planting is nine meters on a crosspatch plan. Control of the ground cover under the trees is desired, but takes planning in advance and attention from the time of establishment to the beginning of full production, which may be a long period. Efforts should be made to keep rodents out of the plantation.

Old plantations are likewise in need of considerable expert attention. They are crowded with vegetation. In several places the palms themselves need to be thinned, since each tree requires a certain amount of light and air and soil area for the accumulation of water. More space is likewise desirable for promotion of resistance to disease and insect pests and for increased production in both quantity and quality of yield. All of this is in line with agricultural practice and attention. In the selection of coconuts for replanting, the general area to be planted should be scouted for superior strains; such selections will have the advantage of acclimatization and probably better adaptation to the local environment.

A survey of coconut palm botany, plant physiology, genetics, nutrition, varietal strains and differences; fungus and virus diseases and insect pests; ground cover in the groves; fertilization; management; drying operations; testing; shelters; and of deterioration in storage and shipping is required so that the copra industry in Micronesia may move into as favorable a place as possible in world production and competition. The present favorable economic prospect will diminish and it will be only with the help of increased yield, reduced cost, and expert management, either native or plantation, that profit will accrue.

An absolute essential to rehabilitation of the copra industry is a dependable transportation system, involving frequent and *regular* scheduled pickups. Another essential – and this applies especially to the larger plantation enterprises – is credit and other assistance in obtaining materials and equipment for clearing plantation lands and drying and storing copra.

Coir fiber, taken from the husk of the coconut, used to be exported to Japan in small quantities and used in the manufacture of rope, brushes, and floor mats. The industry could be revived and would contribute to native income, if a new market were found for it.

Coconut oil, expressed from the nut, offers another source of income. It is used as food and as a component of certain soaps. There is a wide demand for soap in Micronesia, both among natives and foreigners, and no reason why locally produced coconut oil could not supply part of that demand. Some efforts along this line have already been made, but it deserves more vigorous promotion. With assistance provided by the Administration in obtaining and setting up copra presses and soap factories and the necessary materials, natives could engage in this promising industry, as copra and oil manufacturers, as soapmakers, and as merchandisers. Copra-meal cake, a by-product of oil manufacture, could be utilized in the area for livestock food.

2. *Sugar*

The Japanese sugar industry, developed in the Marianas, cannot be revived under present or anticipated conditions. The plantations have been neglected, the installations totally destroyed, and the main source of cheap labor (Okinawan) repatriated. Even if this were not the case, the handicaps of poor terrain and soil, and distance from markets, would render restoration unprofitable except under a system based on cheap and impressed labor, primitive technology, and high government subsidy. For their own part, Micronesians are unsuited and unwilling to undertake the kind of labor that would be required.

3. *Fruits and Vegetables*

Forces garrisoned in Micronesia offer a steady market for native-produced fresh fruits and vegetables, and something along this line is already being done. For the sake of both the native producers and the American consumers, the Administration should give special attention to this enterprise and improve its operation by assisting natives with production and marketing problems.[2] It is ironic that the best markets for such produce exist in Guam and Saipan, where demands on native manpower far exceed supply and where consequently relatively few natives will be induced to undertake commercial farming. Kwajalein, also an important market for produce, is likewise in a predicament; there are no native resources in the Marshalls for producing fruits and vegetables for American consumption, although some consideration should be given to moving Ponape produce to Kwajalein and Majuro by refrigerated vessel.

Rice, in demand for native and garrison forces, was grown in a modest way at Ponape, but natives are neither willing nor suited to undertake the labor involved in large-scale production.

Although soil and climate on some of the high islands may be well suited to the growing of pineapples, a successful development would depend upon a number of factors not likely to obtain, including outside capital, management, and cheap labor, even provided competitive factors permitted profitable operation of such an industry, which is most unlikely.

Prospects for other cash crops depend primarily upon available markets. Cassava, sweet potatoes, castor beans, papain, cotton, coffee, and cacao were formerly dependent upon markets established by Japan. It seems unlikely that a stable and profitable market can be developed for cassava starch, castor beans, or cotton. The supply-and-demand situation in the world today differs so markedly from that created by Japanese economic systems that prospects are not bright for restoring a profitable market for these items. Perhaps cassava may continue to be a source of supplementary starch for the native populations. Cotton also may be used locally, but, in general, island yields are not high and production is believed to be uneconomic. The demand for castor beans is active, but, unless natives find it profitable to produce clean beans at prices approximating levels during the thirties, it does not seem desirable to encourage them. Investigations might be made among natives, especially in the Marianas, to determine if price prospects[3] are sufficiently attractive to interest them.

Papain, the dried milky juice from unripe papaya, was produced on Rota and a few other islands, and production was mostly in the hands of natives. They reported profitable operations. Inquiries should be made to determine whether natives would be interested in producing papain on the basis of about a dollar a pound, in line with prewar American prices. If the reaction is favorable, the Administration should assist producers to restore their prewar positions. (This would be of particular importance to Rota natives, who have few alternative sources of income.)

4. *Forestry*

Present forestry resources of Micronesia will not permit much large-scale exploitation for income purposes. True, the leaves of the pandanus are utilized for handicraft manufacture; but suitable construction timbers are too limited in number and are too scattered to permit economic logging for profit. In some areas there is not even enough lumber to supply local native construction demands. It is recommended that the Administration sponsor a program of forestation, with the following long-term objectives in view:

1. Provision of good construction lumber to supply all native construction needs, thus making them completely independent of lumber imports, whether for building of houses, wharves, native furniture, or boats.
2. Provision of fine cabinet woods for export.
3. Provision of suitable materials for handicraft manufacture.
4. Provision of reserve supplies of breadfruit (for food).
5. Protection of soil from erosion.

In this connection, it is suggested that the Administration avail itself of the experience gained in similar enterprises in other tropical Pacific dependencies. Fiji is a case in point. A long-range program could be worked out by a tropical woods specialist and a forestry expert working together. The forestation program could be incorporated with other government-financed public works rehabilitation programs and would in addition provide income for natives. Priority should be given to initiating the program in areas where natives do not possess many alternative sources of income. (There is good precedent for this kind of enterprise in the CCC program carried out in the United States during the thirties.)

5. *Livestock*

Some thought has been given to initiating enterprises for the production of dairy products and meat for sale to garrison forces and to visiting ships. A small dairy and hog farm now operates on Guam, and it has been proposed that parts of Tinian be converted into a large beef cattle ranch. The Guam project is serving useful purposes and should be maintained, either as an Administration-operated enterprise for direct logistic support of the naval base, or, in time, as a native-owned and -operated business to supply Guam's military and civilian market, or it might be converted into a demonstration farm for training Micronesians in animal husbandry. All three prospects have some value.[4]

The Tinian cattle ranch proposal, on the other hand, is quite another matter. It is unlikely that the garrison forces will undertake to operate a ranch there for their own needs. Also, at present, there are no natives living on Tinian and none available from near-by islands to undertake to acquire and manage such an enterprise, which would require expert assistance and strong financial support from the Administration. It is felt by this Board that any assistance of this sort likely to be available should be concentrated on the more important project of acquiring and distributing livestock to natives for their own subsistence needs. Until these needs are met, it is premature to plan for income-producing enterprises designed primarily to supply meat to the forces.[5]

As an alternative, it has been suggested that some outside company be permitted to acquire land on, say, Tinian and proceed to establish a cattle ranch to provide beef for Guam and Saipan. This Board is not favorable to such a proposal. In the first place, it would involve alienation of Micronesian land by outside interests; although Tinian is at present not occupied by Micronesians, it should be held in reserve for them for future occupation when, as is confidently expected, native population increases. In the second place, at the risk of being labeled dog-in-the-manger, the Board does not favor outsiders' setting up and operating an enterprise which might otherwise eventually be developed by Micronesians.

F. HANDICRAFT

The manufacture of handicraft provides one of the best sources of income for Micronesians and should be encouraged and supported by the Administration. The industry has special importance for those areas which cannot at present secure income from sale of copra or from wages.

In museums throughout the world, Micronesians are noted for their fine hand-woven mats and fans, their facsimile-perfect canoe models, and their delicate tortoise-shell ornaments. The economic iron curtain which Japan drew around most of Micronesia served to enhance the value of the few handicraft articles that managed to get through to western markets.

GI's swept with the force of a storm into the Micronesian scene and in short order bartered the natives out of all their stocks of handicraft plus a good proportion of their household articles and artifacts. Military Government officials restored some order into this commercial chaos by acting as intermediary between native producers and GI purchasers. Handicraft was purchased at standard prices and resold through canteens at cost plus small markups (set aside for native welfare).

While large numbers of naval and military personnel were stationed in the islands, the demand for handicraft far exceeded the supply. At that time most able-bodied natives turned-to and manufactured souvenirs, until, in the case of a few sparsely vegetated atolls, the supplies of weaving material almost ran out. So preoccupied were some communities with this one activity that the Administration made an effort to draw natives back into copra production in order to diversify their source of income and thereby insure them against possible slumps in handicraft markets.

Anticipating the times when local GI markets would no longer be able to absorb the total handicraft output, the Administration attempted to locate markets outside of Micronesia. This was frustrated by government regulations: to the United States government all of Micronesia except Guam was and remains foreign territory. Goods from there, except for "strategic shortages" in products such as copra, are subject to duty, amounting, in the case of handicrafts, to from 30 to 60 per cent ad valorem. Thus penalized, Micronesian handicraft cannot seriously compete pricewise with mass-produced Hawaiian articles which appear to the uncritical purchaser to be almost as good as those from the Marshalls and Carolines.

Until now this market limitation has not affected the handicraft industry. Surpluses produced on the isolated islands are shipped for sale to the Marianas, where naval personnel and their dependents still provide ready markets. The time will come, however, when local demand will decrease and outside markets will have to be developed. Looking forward to that day, and confident in the belief that handicraft can and should be expanded into a major continuing source of income, the Board recommends the following program:

The manufacture and marketing of handicraft should be promoted by the Administration with vigor and imagination. It is too important an income producer to the Micronesians to be left to chance or to inexperienced traders. It is first and foremost a problem in marketing and ought to be managed by an experienced and enthusiastic merchandiser.

Names like Kwajalein, Truk, and Saipan still have sales value to a public which has not yet forgotten all the battlefields of World War II. Also, craftwork – place mats, coasters, carved bowls, tortoise-shell knickknacks, and so forth – is in demand in most large cities. Combine the two factors, and add good selling campaigns, and it seems inescapable that Micronesian handicraft will bring high prices in American markets.

The kinds and quality of articles will, of course, have to be standardized and patterned after market requirements. Once these standards are defined, models could be distributed throughout the islands, and buyers instructed to purchase only reasonably good copies. In this manner native materials and techniques and skills could be adapted to salable objects. It might even prove feasible to establish handicraft classes in vocational schools as did the Japanese and also to train natives to take over buying and exporting functions. The objective would be to assist natives to market their own products in response to competitive bidding.

A prerequisite to expansion of handicraft marketing is removal of American import restrictions. In view of the government's announcement of intentions with regard to Micronesia, it seems academic to continue to maintain that the islands are still "foreign" and their products subject to the customary excessive duties.

Meanwhile, it should be a responsibility of the Administration to insure that natives receive the maximum returns possible from sale of their products. Natives need all the cash they can get to begin restoring their standards of living; the profits they might make, however excessive they may appear to souvenir-hunting amateur economists, will ultimately help along the entire economy to recovery. To this end the Administration should raise handicraft sales prices in local retail outlets to the highest limit the market will bear, and cut down handling markups to a small token percentage. It is considered more important for native craftsmen, and ultimately the whole native community, to receive higher prices for their wares than it is for garrison forces to be able to make purchases at cheap prices.

As a corollary to this proposal, it is recommended that no further effort be made to restrict handicraft production in certain communities just for the sake of encouraging labor to undertake other income enterprises to diversify the economy. Income production, from whatever source, should be encouraged and supported; for the present this is more important than diversification.

Long-range planning for an expanding handicraft industry must consider the need for conserving handicraft raw materials and even for introducing special trees, fibers, and so forth which could be usefully adapted to Micronesian techniques.

From many points of view handicraft production is and could remain the ideal income industry of Micronesia. It can be engaged in by male and female, young and old, working at home and at tempos adapted to native routines. It utilizes native resources and native skills and serves to develop creative talents and healthy pride. And, it offers opportunities for almost complete native management from manufacture to jobbing to exporting.

G. FISHING

1. *Offshore Fishing*

That the offshore fishing resources are considerable will be evident from the fact that by 1937 the Japanese had developed bonito fishing to the extent that it produced 75,000,000 pounds annually, using small craft based at Saipan, Koror, Truk, and Ponape. Several factory ships operating from Japan caught an unknown amount, but a conservative estimate is that the bonito catch totaled in the neighborhood of 100 million pounds. Fishing for tuna began in 1938-39 and was expected to equal bonito in poundage.

Any consideration of deep-sea fishing as a potential source of native income of necessity rests upon the proviso that the fleet is available for catching fish and that plant facilities are on hand to convert fish to a marketable product. The Japanese had facilities both afloat and ashore necessary for the job. They also had trained personnel. They invested millions of yen in floating equipment and shore installations at Saipan, Palau, Truk, and Ponape, the chief areas of exploitation in the Mandated Islands. The South Seas Statistical Yearbook records 762 fishing boats, distributed as follows, for the mandates in 1940:

Island	Fishing Boats
Saipan	183
Yap	15
Palau	239
Truk	180
Ponape	140
Jaluit	5
Total	762

Docks, wharves, sea ways, winches, booms, storage sheds, butchering rooms, refrigeration, power, water, and sundry other essentials were installed on shore. Practically all these are gone. Floating equipment has been reduced to virtually nothing. Also, marketing facilities must be developed again. Latent demand exists, particularly in Japan and the Orient, for the types of products which the islands have produced in the past. Natives are willing, and anxious, to produce fish for export if they can get the equipment for doing so.

Shore installations for drying fish are less expensive than those for canning. Processing, generally speaking, is more simple also, and natives already know some of the elementary techniques and can be trained more easily for developing drying than they can be for operating a canning plant. Rough estimates of essential installations for a minimum setup for producing dried fish on a commercial scale in any area are as follows:

Fleet:	
5 boats - fully equipped, gear, etc., at $20,000 each	$100,000
Ashore:	
Marine ways, winches, etc.	$1,000 to $5,000
Water - source, piping, pumps, etc.	10,000
25-HP steam boiler, installed	5,000
Sheds	5,000
Tables, troughs, washers, etc.	1,000
Drying ovens - 5 at $200 each	1,000
Trays, and incidental interior equipment	1,000
15-ton compressor - 5000 cu. ft. refrigerator	30,000
Box factory	1,000
Estimated total	$155,000 to $159,000

Fishing boats would have to be provided. There were only a few in Saipan, as of midsummer 1946, and only an occasional one in Yap, Palau, Truk, and Ponape. Boats are necessary to supply natives' subsistence needs, to say nothing of producing enough tonnage for processing. Cash income is essential to meet fuel costs even for deep-sea subsistence fishing. Capital expenditure is necessary not only for purchase of floating equipment but also for the shore installations. It seems unlikely that outside private capital will assume not only normal business risks for such uncertain supplies but also additional risks inherent in the present obscure legal status of the islands.[1] Natives need income immediately. They cannot well afford to wait until the peace treaty is signed before any development of fishing is begun. The Administration should begin quickly to provide essential floating equipment and shore installations to help make natives more self-sufficient and to start them on their return to prewar economic levels. Production of dried or salted fish offers possibilities of potential income to natives. Programs should be set up whereby natives can establish a fishing industry in the areas where it previously existed under the Japanese.[2]

Trained personnel who formerly fished in the areas should be brought in under contract to help train native crews and native workers in shore establishments. Types of fishing and processing which were previously carried on are adaptable to the area and its resources.

At Saipan, Palau, Ponape, Kusaie, and Jaluit, native fishermen are eager to engage in offshore fishing, and there can be no question of their ability to do so if given necessary training and initial supervision. The labor supply in the islands could provide the 1250 men needed to operate fifty small fishing vessels, and an additional 250 men and women necessary to handle the shore operations.

Fishing developments as outlined above will employ a greater number and larger proportion of natives than was the case under the Japanese. Previously, natives were employed only sparingly. Some few were hired as fishermen afloat; in general, however, most of this work was done by Japanese. Natives were hired as butchers in the cleaning sheds. Wages for natives in the butchering sheds ran from 40 to 60 yen per month for men during the period around 1940. Rates for women were somewhat less.

2. *Shells*

Trochus shells offer a present source of native income, provided a market can be established. Natives know how to gather trochus shells. They also know where trochus shells were planted by the Japanese. They may need some additional equipment to work the various plantings. Since trochus fishing is a seasonal operation, lasting only a couple of weeks a year, it may be considered as an interim income source, and the amount of income which natives can earn is high for the short period of operation. The Japanese paid 7½ sen per shell for trochus in 1940-41. Approximately 60,000 shells were gathered in Palau in 1941. According to reports, 69,875 kilograms of trochus shells were gathered in the entire mandated area in 1941. These sold for approximately 30 sen per kilo. Trochus shells should yield similar returns for natives again, provided means of distribution and marketing are established. Trochus will provide a year-to-year source of income if appropriate conservation measures are followed.

Pearl oyster shells also grow in the area, and natives know how to gather them. Again, these offer an immediate source of native income which should be fostered. Japanese experiments in culturing pearls were successful at Koror, in the Carolines, and at Ebon, in the Marshalls. The technique for this process can be learned by natives, and the process requires no equipment or facilities not already available. Two years are required to produce cultured pearls, but these can be an extra source of income in connection with regular fishing. Appropriate conservation measures should also be instituted in this case.

3. *Trepang*

Trepang, dried bêche-de-mer, is produced by natives in several islands of the Carolines and Marshalls. Prior to the war this product had a ready market in the Orient. Market prospects are not clear at present and should be investigated. (In this connection it may be pointed out that trepang is already being prepared by natives in the Philippines and exported to China.) Boats are needed, but the number does not reach the proportions or the expense of floating equipment for offshore fishing. Other essential equipment can be supplied largely from local sources. Development of an outlet for the product is the chief problem to be settled.

4. *Other Marine Products*

Tortoise shells, cowrie shells, and sponges are produced in some islands. Production of these items usually is considered a part of the general fishing activity and not as separate industries. Natives use tortoise shells in handicraft manufacture and also for sale as shells. Income from tortoise shells is relatively small, in general accounting for a minor part of natives' income in any area. Markets for tortoise shells should receive additional investigation. Appropriate conservation measures for development of a steady supply of tortoise shell are desirable and require attention.

Markets for ornamental shells should be established to provide profitable outlets for native production. Income from sale of ornamental shells in general does not offer great prospects, but additional income from whatever source is desirable.

Sponges were planted in some of the outer islands by the Japanese, but are not as yet produced in commercial quantities. Possibilities of developing commercial sponge production merits investigation with respect both to suitable types and market outlets.

5. *Research*

Based on the belief that research constitutes a most important factor in any fisheries program, the recommendation is made that the Administration enlist the aid of the appropriate Federal agency in setting up a research program. The Japanese recognized the need of research as a basis for exploitation and established a modern fisheries experiment station at Koror, Palaus, in 1932, with three survey vessels for offshore work. This station had outdoor pools supplied with running sea water for observation of living marine organisms; biological and bacteriological laboratories; technological equipment for processing, freezing, and storing seafood; machine and carpenter shops for construction and testing of fishing gear; and a museum for public educational purposes. A similar institution in the United States would cost at least $100,000.

There is no intention of suggesting that the Japanese regarded their investment in marine fisheries experiments as being primarily for the good of the natives; on the contrary, it was to protect and extend capital earnings. The net result, however, was to increase native income through such indirect means as higher levels of employment in related businesses.

Under United States administration, it is expected that native income will be derived from participation in fisheries enterprises, so research should be of direct benefit to them, as well as supplying basic information for the United States fisheries generally. Because of its cost and wide application, research is everywhere considered a proper function of government.

H. MINING

The principal economic mineral products of Micronesia in order of importance are phosphate, bauxite, and manganese. Smaller amounts of copper, iron, zinc, bat guano, asbestos, and gold are known and have been more or less systematically prospected, and there are repeated but unconfirmed rumors of the occurrence of nickel and silver.

Phosphate is by all odds the most important and the most widely distributed mineral resource in Micronesia. During the period of Japanese occupation, deposits were mined on the following islands: Angaur, Peleliu, Tobi, Sonsorol, Fais, Gaferut, Rota, Tinian, Saipan, Ebon, and possibly a few others. In addition, small phosphate deposits are known on Fana, Kapingamarangi, Ngatik, Aguijan, Medenilla, Bikar, and a few other small islands. The grade of the material varies from as high as 40 per cent P_2O_5 for some of the material from Angaur to material which is better classed as phosphatic clay. During the period of Japanese occupation, 2,985,975 metric tons of phosphatic material were mined and shipped to the home islands for conversion to superphosphate. Most of this material appears to have been used in Japan proper; there were some relatively small shipments sent to the islands for the sugar industry.

American bombs and shells totally wrecked Japanese phosphate installations, including rail lines, drying plants, storage sheds, and loading devices, so that any revival of mining operations would entail rebuilding from the ground up – a thoroughly uneconomic enterprise because of the paucity of unmined phosphate still remaining.

Small stockpiles of mined but undried material of various grades, estimated to contain a total of 215,000 metric tons, remain on Angaur, Tobi, Sonsorol, Fais, and Rota. The acute fertilizer shortage in Japan moved SCAP to arrange for this mined material to be shipped to Japan. An American contracting firm has undertaken this project and is now engaged in cleaning out the stockpiles and is even considering reviving mining operations. Their contractual arrangement with the government permits this otherwise uneconomic project to be undertaken profitably – for the firm if not for the government. Work supervision is under Americans, and most of the labor is carried out by Japanese brought in for the purpose. A few local natives only are employed.

This project is very worth while – for Japan. For Micronesia it is unmitigated exploitation. Micronesian soils are notably poor in quality; when the press of population someday forces more intensive cultivation, there will develop a need for the very phosphate which is now being stripped off the land and sent away. Further, mined-out phosphate areas are transformed from fertile garden sites to useless, sterile land;

Micronesian land is too limited to tolerate this. The project is highhanded in another respect: a highly valuable *Micronesian* natural resource is being exported, without profit to Micronesians. It is true that records are being kept of exports, with a remote possibility that the proceeds may someday, someway, be utilized for Micronesia; but the Micronesian owners – and who can put forward stronger claims for ownership than they? – need income now, and severance fees should be paid to them for their loss of a valuable natural resource. As it now stands, except for a few local natives presently engaged and, incidentally, drawing discriminatory wages, the present phosphate project does not provide an income source for the large number of natives eager for employment. There is, notwithstanding, one useful by-product resulting from this project: company representatives, having been given a relatively free hand, have conducted their relations with the native inhabitants so awkwardly and unfeelingly that this case may serve as a warning to the Administration to discourage similar exploitative enterprises in the future.

In the light of these circumstances alternative recommendations are offered, with preference in favor of the first one:

1. Stop immediately the export of phosphate stockpiles and undertake no mining. Insure that native owners promptly receive royalties for all phosphate already exported since occupation by the United States. Undertake to fill Japan's needs from other sources (for example, from Florida, which could probably provide a less expensive supply). Retain all phosphate, including stockpiles, in site for future use in Micronesia.
2. Undertake to fill Japan's urgent phosphate needs from sources outside Micronesia, but, while revision in plans is being accomplished, continue to ship stockpiled ore from Angaur, Tobi, and Sonsorol to Japan. Undertake no mining operations. Utilize local natives instead of imported Japanese for labor and pay them equitable wages; this will serve as a source, temporary, to be sure, of badly needed income. Administration officials will serve as intermediaries in all relations between company and natives. (This alternative is less desirable than the first and is to be considered only under the circumstances that phosphate is not immediately available from other sources and that high policy rules that Japan's needs are more important than Micronesia's.)

Sometime in the future Micronesians will need their phosphate resources for agricultural purposes. It is completely within the realm of possibility that they will then be capable of organizing their own mining and processing enterprises, to provide for Micronesia's needs with a relatively cheap local product. In this manner maximum benefits will accrue to Micronesians whether they be owners, manufacturers, or consumers.[1]

Bauxite deposits are confined to, but are not necessarily coëxtensive with, the high islands in the former mandated area, that is, those islands which expose a core of basic igneous rocks. The principal production, in fact the only production of any commercial importance, was from the mines at Ngardmau on the northern end of Babelthuap in the Palau group. In addition, deposits were prospected on Saipan, Yap, Ponape, and Kusaie. It is reported that a small tonnage of bauxite was mined and shipped from Ponape, but this has not been confirmed. Bauxitic material has been reported from Rota, and the presence of bauxite on Guam was determined in the course of this Survey. The discovery of bauxite in the Mandated Islands occurred about 1937, and the total production during the period of Japanese occupation was approximately 400,000 metric tons, of which 369,227 came from the mines at Ngardmau.

The Japanese estimated proven reserves on Babelthuap at 2,000,000 tons, on Yap 6,000 tons, and on Ponape 400,000 tons. No estimates are available for tonnages on Kusaie, Saipan, and Guam. The figures for Babelthuap represent "measured ore," and the potential reserves are much larger.

The grade of the bauxite is uniformly good. Average analyses run between 52 per cent and 55 per cent Al_2O_3, 3 per cent to six per cent SiO_2, and between 10 per cent and 20 per cent Fe_2O_3.

Only those bauxite deposits on northern Babelthuap appear to be of possible commercial importance to the United States at the present time. The material is somewhat different in its chemical and physical properties from that which is now being refined in the United States and its use may require special treatment. A stockpile of washed material containing 20,000 to 25,000 tons is available at the mine and on the pier and can be moved without undue expense. If shipping charges to West Coast ports are not unduly high, and if this material can be processed without requiring extensive plant modifications, it is possible that this deposit could be profitably exploited.

Unlike the phosphate deposits, the mining of bauxite in Babelthuap will not seriously interfere with native agriculture.

Palau natives would like to see a revival of bauxite mining on Babelthuap. Under Japanese management they were employed as laborers and as minor supervisors at relatively high wages. Native communities profited from income derived from the work, and because of enlightened Japanese recruitment and labor policies, native community life was not disrupted. Wages were paid either on a time or a piece basis, according to the habits and preferences of the workers.

It is recommended that serious consideration be given to the revival of bauxite mining on Babelthuap. (Although this is of no direct concern to this Survey, it is tempting to suggest that our government may ultimately benefit by stockpiling offshore bauxite in the United States as an emergency reserve.) It is proposed that the Administration invite outside capital and management to undertake the enterprise, subject to the following conditions: that native ownership (whether individual or communal) be acknowledged and that owners be paid prospecting fees, mining leases, and severance fees for all ore mined; that native labor be utilized to the fullest extent possible, with provisions for more capable natives to be advanced to responsible positions, and that wages be based on work rather than on ethnic status; and that the Administration act as intermediary between company and native communities and maintain constant scrutiny over relations between company and native employees.

Small deposits of manganese minerals were mined on Saipan, Rota, Guam and Yap. The total production of the islands is unknown, but probably did not exceed 5,000 tons of hand-picked concentrates. None of the deposits seen during the Survey appears to be of commercial importance and does not constitute a source of income for natives.

Iron and copper and possibly asbestos have been mined in small amounts on Yap. None of these appears to be of economic importance; but the occurrence of copper on Yap merits further study because of the possibility that its exploitation may offer a source of income to local natives.

Deposits of limonite were mined in the vicinity of Metalanim on Ponape and were smelted to form a crude ferrosilicon. The extent of these deposits is not known and the industry was not large. The so-called gold mine on the southeastern coast of Babelthuap shows very little gold but a fair amount of sphalerite and chalcopyrite. Traces of gold have been reported on Ponape and on Truk, but the amounts were so small that no attempt was made to work the deposits.

Small deposits of bat guano are found on practically all of the islands which are high enough to possess caves. Most important deposits are on Kusaie, Ponape, and various islands in the Palau area. The mining of these deposits has never assumed more than local importance; nevertheless, they constitute sources of valuable fertilizer and should be reserved for that purpose locally.

I. BUSINESS ENTERPRISES

The natives of Micronesia, for the first time in the history of their association with foreign economies, are now in a position to demonstrate the real potentiality of their own skill and organization in the field of business enterprise. In past years, the Spaniards, the Germans, and the Japanese, and even the Americans in Guam, have retained almost exclusive control of economic resources in Micronesia and have exploited them to their own advantage, depending on the native population as a source of cheap labor. The need to rehabilitate the Micronesians at a time when the whole world is faced with shortages and priorities demands the fullest utilization of resources within the islands; not the least of these resources is the ability of Micronesians to control and manage their own economic enterprises if provided with support and encouragement from the Administration. Their unfortunate habits of deference and self-deprecation, learned through years of regimentation under other administrators, must be eradicated by education and training to allow full play for the latent capabilities which the natives possess and which are needed now to forward their rehabilitation and economic independence.

As individuals, the natives have developed a number of home industries, such as wood carving, weaving, mat and basket making, shell handicraft, and the making of cordage and fishnets, but the marketing of produce has usually been in the hands of non-natives. Many opportunities for business enterprise have been provided by the islands' resources, such as mining, forest products, commercial fishing, processing of marine products, copra and other agricultural production, cordage manufacture, shell industries, animal husbandry, poultry farming, and miscellaneous food and manufacturing industries, but again the foreigner generally cornered the management and the profits. In the mandated area, the Japanese invested large sums in terms of capital goods and organization, particularly in the Marianas and the Palaus, less in Yap and the low islands eastward. Great companies, controlled by the Japanese government or by powerful families in Japan, provided the organization and reaped the profits. However, the intensive colonization of the mandated area by Japanese and Okinawans and the resulting concentration of population provided some Micronesians with advantages which they could only receive in association with urban settlement - electric lights, running water, wider range of imported goods, and, most of all, opportunities for income beyond that which their own environment could provide. Thus, a sizable number of highly profitable small enterprises developed, and natives competed with Japanese in managing drygoods shops, butcher shops, fish markets, drug stores, restaurants, hotels, public baths, laundries, bakeries, shoe-repair shops, taxi services, barber shops, and dressmaking establishments, catering mainly to the Japanese population.

In most of the islands, outside the Marianas, there was little development of occupational organization along lines of a capitalistic economy, with its specialists and entrepreneurs. Managers of small businesses, who were more often Japanese than native, usually operated as individuals, but in a few instances they were incorporated. In Palau, the Japanese introduction of the *kumiai*, or business association, was well received by Palauans. Only natives were eligible for membership in the *kumiai*, participation was voluntary, and leadership was provided by high chiefs who determined policy in consultation with Japanese officials. A number of associations were organized, each one designed to include a specific economic group, such as market producers, commercial farmers, copra growers, ferry operators, charcoal makers, barbers, lumber mill operators, carpenters, and trepang fishers. The *kumiai* performed a number of necessary economic functions: they set the prices of commodities and services; consumers were protected through the enforcement of health regulations, safety precautions, and minimum standards in quality of workmanship; licenses were issued by the association to new businesses; farmers' produce was collected by association ships and transported to markets; native produce was allocated so that all sections of the population would be insured sufficient unto their need; goods were insured against disaster; and credit was extended to good risks. The funds for the establishment of each *kumiai* were contributed by the members of the association.

Big business in the mandated area was completely in the control of a few Japanese corporations. *Nanyo Kohatsu Kaisha* (South Seas Development Company) resulted from the amalgamation of two Japanese firms in 1921. Its capitalization increased from an initial three million yen to forty million yen by 1938. More than 50 per cent of the original shares were held by the powerful Oriental Exploitation Company, which continued to hold the controlling interest in the development of the sugar industry on Saipan, the phosphate production on Peleliu and Tobi, and a number of subsidiary activities such as ice manufacture, shipbuilding, fishing, and agricultural enterprises throughout the Carolines. In the decade just prior to the war, *Nanyo Takushoku Kaisha* (South Seas Exploitation Company) assumed a leading role in the development of resources in the mandated area. Founded in 1936 with an initial capitalization of twenty million yen, this company received mining rights and properties in phosphate on Angaur and Fais from the South Seas government in return for a majority interest in the stock; other principal investors were the big families of Japanese business. While *Nanyo Takushoku Kaisha* was primarily interested in the mining of phosphates, it also managed directly more than twenty affiliated or subsidiary companies engaged in such activities in the mandated area as bauxite mining, pineapple raising, pearl fishing, and processing of marine products. Its activities were restricted almost entirely to the Carolines. *Nanyo Boeki Kaisha* (South Seas Trading Company) was principally dominant in the eastern Carolines and the Marshalls. Formed as early as 1906, it became active in the area even during the German period and fell heir to the extensive interests of the Jaluit Company in 1914. Effective control of the company's stock was held by the Kawasaki family, one of the leading banking and industrial families of Japan. The company operated the major steamship lines connecting the outlying islands, maintained agents on most of the islands and atolls, bought nearly all copra for export, and brought the majority of imported goods into the islands. It was subsidized in these enterprises by the South Seas Bureau. Other Japanese companies had interests in the fields of shipping, bauxite mining, lumbering, and radio-telephone service. All non-Japanese companies which had operated in the islands previously had withdrawn by 1922, since which time foreign commercial interests in the area have been practically nonexistent.

On prewar Guam, the native inhabitants held an economic position somewhat analogous to that of their fellows on Saipan, but under the control of American business interests established on Guam or operating from the States. Representatives of American companies were generally Americans, although Guamians participated in this aspect of business to a small extent. Guamian agricultural production and trade was for the most part owned and controlled on an individual or family basis. Within their own communities, individuals operated stores, poolrooms, taxi services; a few natives leased land and houses to American personnel stationed on Guam; and several enterprising Guamians managed small industries, such as the soap factory and tile factory which, however, were only a small part of the island's total economy. Naval interests dominated the scene, the Bank of Guam was owned by the Navy, and the island economy was oriented to satisfy the needs of some 1500 naval personnel based at the naval station.

The war has created a vacuum in the economy of the Mandated Islands by the withdrawal of Japanese civilian workers and financial assets in yen currency and by the destruction of vast quantities of capital equipment formerly controlled and operated by Japanese corporations and entrepreneurs. The natives are anxious to revive many prewar enterprises and to expand their activities into fields vacated by the Japanese, but their funds have been dissipated in the depreciation of the yen and they lack adequate equipment to begin operations. At present, almost the only native business enterprise is trading, although in some areas artisans, farmers, fishermen, and boatbuilders are being assisted on an individual basis by the Administration. Trading has been established in most islands through coöperative stores which buy their trade goods from the United States Commercial Company. This is working out fairly successfully as an emergency operation, but many natives hope eventually to own their business enterprises individually rather than collectively. Going a step further, natives should be encouraged and assisted in taking over most of the commercial functions now carried out by the United States Commercial Company.[1]

In Palau, natives wish to revive the *kumiai* associations in order to control their own economy along lines they had begun to learn before the war. They ask whether their funds, frozen in Japanese trust deposits, can be made available so that they might buy equipment to resume operations. On Saipan, natives have formed associations which now own their own fishing vessels and which as a group sell their produce to the Administration. They, too, need more vessels and shore facilities for processing their catch if they are to expand their activities. In other places, copra production, carried out along traditional lines of individual or family organization, will continue to be almost the only commercial enterprise in which natives can engage. Where the concentrations of Japanese populations before the war have now disappeared, and with them the advantages of urban settlement formerly enjoyed by adjacent native communities, there are still business opportunities among the native population and in connection with concentrations of American service personnel and civilians.

On Guam, the situation appears brighter for native economic advancement, for Guamians have both capital (over three million dollars in the Bank of Guam) and labor resources for business enterprise. While their return even to prewar standards has been retarded by failure thus far to reëstablish mainland business connections and transport facilities, as well as shortages in the world market for consumers' goods and durable goods, there has been an increase of Americans on Guam from the prewar figure of 1,500 to 30,000 at the present. This American community, which surpasses the 25,000 natives in number, is a windfall for Guamian entrepreneurs who are able to satisfy the demands of Americans in the usual adjuncts of civilization – drug stores, gasoline stations, beauty shops, taxi service, and numerous other small businesses. The problem, therefore, is not one of capital, or labor, or market for goods and services, but of management. While many Americans believe that Guamians lack the necessary managerial ability to meet the new situation, there is no reason why groups of Guam businessmen, with the necessary capital, cannot hire American management for their enterprises, in the same way that mainland firms formerly hired American management to represent their interests on Guam.[2]

Native control of local business enterprise should be encouraged and given practical assistance as a desirable objective by means of which a greater measure of native self-sufficiency may be insured and native economic welfare advanced through retention by natives of the benefits of business activity.

The institutional form of native economic enterprise should be adapted to the cultural background and the current wishes of the islanders. In some areas, appropriate economic organization may assume the characteristics of private enterprise, whereas in other areas the basis for business organization may rest in the community and assume a coöperative character. However, neither type of institutional organization should be used exclusively unless there is conclusive evidence that the types of organization excluded are foreign to native thinking and practices. In general, the principle that each type of economic organization is complementary should be fostered.

Concentration of economic control in the hands of a few natives should not be encouraged as a permanent policy. Ownership of the instruments of native economic control should be distributed on a broad basis among natives. The promotion of a broad basis for ownership of the instruments of economic control should be designed to discourage tendencies toward undesirable monopoly and to promote the benefits of competition.

Government regulation of native-operated enterprises should be held to the minimum necessary to ensure equity and freedom from exploitation. Where licensing may be necessary, it should be restricted to matters of public health and safety and in the interest of conservation; it should by no means serve as a hindrance to free competion.

The distribution of finished goods should be placed as soon as possible and feasible in the hands of native-operated enterprises. The form of enterprise should be determined in accordance with traditional practices and local conditions.

Where natives have within their control the potential investment, capital, and labor sufficient to organize and operate economic enterprises to satisfy the demands of expanded

American communities in the islands, but where they generally lack management ability owing to inexperience and have inadequate mainland connections, special assistance should be provided whereby native investors may have access to mainland reservoirs of managerial talent qualified for specific types of business or for handling relatively large-scale economic enterprises. Such special technical assistance should be employed on a contract basis by Guamians who require the service in the successful operation of their enterprises.

In some cases, consideration may be given to the entrance of outside enterprise to facilitate the development of the islands' economic resources and to augment the income of the native population; however, careful safeguards should be established to avoid any exploitation of natives or their resources.

Where the *kumiai*, or business association, was of direct benefit to the native economy and where the natives wish to revive it, the *kumiai* should be reëstablished as soon as possible, supervision being shared by native chiefs and administrative officials to ensure sound and equitable business practices. Wherever the principle of the *kumiai* would be useful and appropriate in coöperative ventures elsewhere in the islands, it might be used as a pattern of organization.

Native enterprises should be assisted by provision of capital goods either through importation from available sources outside of the islands or from stockpiles of military materials in the islands. Further assistance should be given in the releasing of native assets from frozen funds and in the extension of credit to enterprises which will aid in the rehabilitation of native economy.

Notes

B. INCOME LEVELS

1. All monetary figures in this paragraph given on the basis of four yen to the dollar.

2. This recommendation has been acted upon to a gratifying degree; and although the final goal of "like wages for like work" has not yet been attained anywhere, the Administration appears to be very conscious of its desirability and to be moving in that direction.

3. By 1949 many of the inequities described here and below had been corrected. Prices paid for native products were considerably higher; incentive goods and tools of production were more numerous and less expensive; and copra exports had greatly increased. The Administration has pushed these economic reforms with vigor.

C. UNPAID CLAIMS

1. The Administration now (1949) has on file most claims coming under the above categories, but up to the present no adjudication of such claims has taken place outside of Guam.

D. LABOR

1. By 1949 most of these abuses had been corrected.

2. Most of the recommendations listed in this section have received favorable endorsement, and many of them have been acted upon. Job classification has been systematized, wage scales equated, hours regularized, away-from-home employment restricted, and native laborers generally protected from more obvious abuses.

E. AGRICULTURE AND FORESTRY

1. There has been vast improvement in copra production since 1946. Price to natives has risen to $80 a ton, and during the first six months of 1948 alone over five thousand

tons were sold to the Island Trading Company for marketing on the mainland.

2. In place of this, the Administration has recently leased nearly a thousand acres on Tinian to three Americans to grow vegetables for sale to garrison forces in the Marianas. Some natives work as laborers on this project.

3. The average price between 1930 and 1940 was $47.69 per long ton; the range was from $37.41 to $68.77.

4. The Guam stock farm has been maintained and serves as a demonstration center as well as a source of stock for improving native herds and flocks.

5. Most of the Tinian livestock was subsequently distributed throughout the Territory as a rehabilitation measure.

G. FISHING

1. Contrary to this expectation, several American companies have expressed an interest in starting fishing enterprises in the Trust Territory, and the United States government has issued a regulation permitting such enterprises - subject, however, to strict controls which insure safeguarding of natives' interests.

2. Subsequently, the Administration assisted a group of Carolinians residing on Saipan to organize the Saipan Fishing Company. The company operates several sampans and sells its catches on Saipan and Guam.

H. MINING

1. Higher authority compelled the Naval Administration to permit continued exploitation of the Angaur deposits, including even the resumption of mining operations. Some royalties have been collected on exports, presumably for partial compensation to Angaur natives for their loss of this valuable resource.

I. BUSINESS ENTERPRISES

1. This paragraph requires considerable revision in the light of developments since 1946. The Administration has actively sponsored native business enterprises, and at Guam and Saipan, at least, such native-owned and -operated businesses are more numerous than they were before the war. Also, subsequent to the Survey, the United States Commercial Company and its successor, the Island Trading Company, have in fact turned over most retail trade units to native ownership and operation.

2. Since this was written native businessmen on Guam have progressed far toward building up and managing their own enterprises; this has involved direct contacts with mainland firms.

CHAPTER IV. INSTITUTIONAL NEEDS

A. WEIGHTS AND MEASURES

Various systems of weights and measures have been introduced to Micronesian custom by previous and present administrations, as well as by passing traders. Some acquaintance by islanders with systems of weights and measures from the Occident, the Orient, and from local sources may be found throughout the area. However, the metric system is more widely known throughout the area than any other. It was introduced to the islands by the Spanish in the nineteenth century and used as a basis for commercial transactions and for land measurements by both the Spanish and the Germans. Most islanders are acquainted with kilograms, liters, hectares, meters, and their various subdivisions and multiples.

The Japanese administration used the metric system of weights and measures also, particularly in purchases of raw materials and in the sale of many consumers' goods. They also introduced the Japanese system of weights and measures, but the metric system continued to be the main basis for exchange transactions between islanders and Japanese, especially for large quantities. Several cadastral surveys of the Mariana Islands and other areas were undertaken by the Japanese. They introduced the *cho* as a basic unit of land measurement. The *cho* equals .9917 hectares or 2.4505 acres, hence it approximates the basic unit of land measurement in the metric system. Specific, permanent boundary markers were established by the Japanese in their land surveys. Ownership was established and titles were based thereon in many instances. Many of these boundary markers remain. Additional surveys may well use the formerly established boundary markers as a basis for relocation and reëstablishment of land measurements.

The metric system should be maintained as a legal system of weights and measures in the islands. The metric system is a legal system within the United States, although the United States system is much more widely used as a matter of custom. The custom in the islands rests more upon the metric system than upon any other system. It is recommended that the metric system should be maintained insofar as practicable, allowing use of the United States system but not forcing its use. Trading with islanders should be upon the metric system. Scales and other measures for trading should designate both the metric and the United States systems in order to facilitate clear understanding between each party to the transaction. Land measurements should follow the metric system, subject to the slight modifications which have been introduced by previous recent surveys.

B. FINANCE

1. *Monetary Units and Circulating Media*

The United States dollar has been established as, and should continue to be, the basic monetary unit for commercial exchange throughout the Mariana, Caroline, and Marshall Islands.

Specie is the form of circulating media generally preferred by natives, particularly in outer islands. Hard money has numerous advantages to natives especially in isolated areas. Their preference for money forms should receive favorable consideration.

Use among natives of stone, shell, or other forms of native money should not be controlled or prohibited. Native moneys frequently have significance beyond western concepts of exchange. Often the full value of native money cannot be determined, any more than quantitative values can be placed upon heirlooms, family silver, or china in occidental cultures. Administrators should be careful not to rule such factors out of the native culture, especially when their full significance is not completely known.

Foreigners, including all American personnel, should not be allowed to buy native money or to trade with natives in local exchange media.

2. *Monetary Control*

The volume of basic monetary media in circulation should not be controlled by formal administrative action if the total amount of exportable goods and wage payments to natives are reasonably well balanced by imports of goods meeting native requirements. It is a regrettable but well-established fact that the volume of imported goods available for native purchase is now much less than the natives want and need. Concerted efforts should be given to increasing imports of essential goods for native use not only to satisfy better basic requirements but also to relieve price pressures upon current sales. Measures for promoting natives' savings may be fostered also, if the possibility of increasing imports sufficiently to prevent undue inflationary price trends appears remote. The extent of natives' output, that is, surplus production and services for wages, should largely determine the volume of circulating media in natives' hands. The amount of trade goods and other available materials (plus prices) will largely determine the rate of money turnover.

3. *Prices and Fiscal Policy*

The Administration has established, and presumably will continue to establish, basic prices to natives for imported goods and exports. Apart from military orders, or any other authoritative regulations, prices to natives of imports and of exports are in fact controlled by (a) monopoly operation of the supplier (Military Government and United States Commercial Company) and (b) the general inability of native consumers to obtain supplies from alternative sources and by native producers to find alternative market outlets. So long as this situation occurs, more consideration should be given to natives' bargaining power, the amount of labor necessary to buy goods, alternative sources of cash income, and alternative types of production.[1]

If the supply of goods and outlets available to individual purchasers, or the number of outlets available to individual sellers, offers effective competition *in fact*, it is unnecessary to control prices in local channels of trade by formal administrative action. Such is not the case in 1946. Price controls adapted to local situations should be retained with respect to distribution of imports at local levels until competition establishes stable markets. Difficulties of establishing and obtaining effective and *equitable* levels of prices are all too obvious. Administrators should confer with chiefs and other responsible natives to arrive at the most equitable prices for goods moving in trade within local communities. The need for price control, the determination of particular prices, and methods of control should be scrutinized constantly; prices and price controls should be formally reviewed and analyzed periodically, at least every six months and preferably more often.

Native societies may wish to maintain price controls in conformity with their customs. They should be authorized to do so subject to approval by the Administration.

4. *Basic Prices*

A basing point for price determination should be established. It may be the price paid for goods purchased or sold at usual mainland markets. Pricing policy with respect to the insufficient supply of goods now moving into Micronesia is based in general upon purchase price plus an average markup. Distinctions should be made between pricing policies for ordinary consumers' goods, production goods, semidurable goods, and capital goods. Consideration should be given in establishing pricing policies to variations in natives' basic requirements. These variations may arise from many different causes, not the least of which might be the complete destruction of former productive facilities and capital goods by combat. Consideration should also be given to natives' ability to purchase goods within limits of their present incomes and, in addition, to the comparability of natives' present income and price levels with former income and purchasing power.

5. *Consumers' Goods*

Consumers' goods, such as staple foods, textiles, variety goods, etc., may be priced in the islands on the basis of cost at outgoing mainland port plus distribution costs. Possible exceptions may be considered if additional consumption of specific goods is required for native welfare. If, for example, additional consumption of canned or dried milk is desired for infants, such a program might be considered as part of a special welfare program. Also, if natives are in dire need of specific items, it may be necessary to qualify price policy accordingly for such goods. In general, however, if a basis is to be laid for a competitive economy within native control, pricing policy on consumers' goods should follow cost at outgoing port plus distribution.

6. *Consumers' Durable or Productive Goods*

Consumers' durable goods or goods which enable natives to increase their own production should be priced on a basis similar to that just previously expressed, subject to some important qualifications. Consumers' durable or production goods may be priced on the basis of export market plus *or minus* margins which tend to equate average native income-price relationships during the 1936 to 1940 period. If such items as knives, adzes, pots, fish nets, chickens, hogs, cattle, or nails cost a day's labor for a given unit in the 1936 to 1940 period, a similar unit of the same product should be procurable now for a day's wage. Perhaps the wage may be adjusted more readily in some instances; in others the price should be lowered; or, perhaps a combination of adjustments should be used to accomplish the objective. The main objective is to get goods into natives' hands which will enable them to increase their own production and thereby help themselves and, at the same time, save expenses on the part of the governing power. A corollary objective is to provide natives with these categories of goods at prices, or wage-and-product expenditures, similar to those before the war. Consumers' durable or production goods should be as directly comparable as possible in quality to similar goods which served native requirements before the war. When directly comparable goods are not available, appropriate adjustments in price should apply. It is most important, however, that quality of consumers' durable goods now offered for sale to natives should not be less favorable than prewar qualities. Natives already know, or soon learn, which are better quality steels, textiles, or other items with which they work every day. Shoddy merchandise is not welcomed by them, even at discounts.

7. *Capital Goods*

Capital goods may be priced on a mainland or area of production basis, *less* sufficient margin – usually substantial – which will allow natives to purchase within their ability to pay. Capital goods, such as boats, cement, engines, oil presses, lumber, and so forth, involve relatively large expenditures that contribute to natives' standards of living over a long period of time. With most capital installations gone and with native savings at an extreme low, special consideration should be given to making essential capital installations for rehabilitation of native economy. These should be undertaken without delay. Considerations of natives' ability to pay for such installations may involve, among other considerations, current income, natives' savings, the effect of the size of deferred payments upon native income, and the effect of the introduction of such capital installations upon production for native use. In numerous instances, where the introduction or reintroduction of capital goods into the native economy will have beneficial effects upon native production, prices of capital goods should be only a *token* portion of original cost. In some instances, the cost of capital investments may be borne entirely and directly by the government, with later assumption of partial costs, or costs of operation, by native groups or organizations. Such a practice would be similar to that which is frequently followed by Chambers of Commerce seeking new business for their communities.

8. *Export Prices*

Price policies for exportable commodities should be based upon the principle that natives are to receive the greatest amount of return possible for their goods which is commensurate with sound distribution practices. Prices to natives for their products should be stable. Natives do not react favorably to fluctuating prices, particularly falling prices, any better than do producers in any other part of the world. At present, it may be more desirable for marketing agencies to take a somewhat larger margin than normal upon the basis of high world price levels, but if that is done, the operating agencies should be prepared to reduce their margins when world market prices decline so that prices to natives may be held as nearly as possible to steady levels. Organizations of natives should be promoted to market their own products so that they will not only try to develop less costly and more efficient marketing methods but also so that they may secure larger proportions of their sale price. Prices for exports should be based on outgoing port from Micronesia, presumably Guam, until local organizations are developed to carry marketing through to world markets. Differentials may be established among the islands to cover necessary transportation and other essential costs among the islands to outgoing port. Such differentials, if any, should be established only on actual cost basis and not on hypothetical costs, that is, there should be no extra charge for added distances unless the carrier actually charges more.

9. *Sources for Financing*

The Administration must offer financial assistance to develop successful enterprise in Micronesia. Former administrations were forced to follow such a policy, especially the Japanese. The development of economic enterprise in the area for purposes of exporting practically any commodity, except copra, involves relatively large capital investment, comparatively small production of goods in terms of world trade, vast distances, difficult transportation problems, and unique marketing procedures. Outside financial assistance will be necessary for successfully developing native economic enterprises, except perhaps for some activities whose productions are intended entirely for local use. Most goods which can be produced successfully in Micronesia are also produced in relatively large volume in markets readily available to the United States. The nature and magnitude of American demand for raw materials and finished or semifinished products formerly produced in the islands differ sufficiently from previous demand factors to operate against revival of many former industries on the same scale. However, some industries offer reasonable prospects of success if organized on somewhat different scales of magnitude and under alternative types of control and organization. Industries, such as production of dried fish, may be revived in native hands, with proper guidance and management to get them started. Capital installations will be required. These must be financed. It seems inescapable that the governing power must offer the financial assistance for reviving this industry, or others which offer similar problems, if these activities are to become productive again.

Financial assistance may be granted in several ways: (1) by assumption of complete cost of capital installations and management expenses until an enterprise is able to carry on by itself; (2) by absorption of losses resulting from trade especially in production and capital goods; and (3) by direct payments to induce specific activity along desired lines.

During the period of native economic recovery and rehabilitation, the interpretation of "capital installations" should be relatively broad wherever proposed projects contribute directly to increasing native production and income. The ultimate cost of supporting the native economy may be less if natives are assisted immediately in promoting their self-support. They are anxious to engage in enterprise which makes them more self-sufficient. They have confidence in their ability to do so. These positive factors should be recognized and stimulated.

Additions to native output and self-sufficiency will be considerable in numerous instances where desirable production of capital goods, such as small tools, livestock, fishing boats, and so forth, can be placed in their hands immediately. Generally, natives should have full title to these items. In many cases natives are unable at present to pay full current market prices for them. These items should be sold to natives in accordance with their ability to pay during the interim period of readjustment. Losses incurred in trade on these items should be borne by the Administration.

Replanting of coconuts, revegetation of certain areas, or greater production of other crops may be appropriate and desirable programs in some areas. If specific programs along these lines are considered in the best interests of natives and still they do not have the means at present for carrying through on them, or if additional production is desired for other good reasons, direct payments may be made to natives for their participation in building up their own resources along lines which ultimately will mean less drain upon the Administration.

Which agency assumes responsibility for financial assistance along the above-mentioned lines is a matter for executive determination. However, the agency which has over-all responsibility over natives' welfare may be expected to bear this cost, unless specific circumstances dictate otherwise in particular cases. It is particularly desirable, in the interests of better administration, that responsibility for over-all fiscal aid be centralized in order to maintain coördinated and balanced programs.[2]

10. *Duties on Micronesian Products*

Import duties which have applied to goods shipped to the United States from the former Mandated Islands should be removed. Present duties impose a burden upon trade with the area. A preferential status with the United States is desirable if trade between the islands and the mainland is to become a reality. The total amount of materials and goods which now originates from this area is comparatively small. Their importance to the native economy are in inverse proportion to their importance to the United States. It is recommended that United States import duties on all goods, especially handicraft and raw materials, originating in the area should be removed without delay.

11. *Finance and Wages*

The extent and type of economic activities supported by the Administration will determine largely the degree to which the objective of native incomes, favorably comparable to prewar years, can be attained. In areas still suffering heavily from combat damage, programs should be sponsored which are designed to rehabilitate the native economy and to promote native self-sufficiency. Assuming average constant employment, wage rates paid by the Administration or by other sources will tend to direct the flow of labor into certain channels. Programs for promotion of native rehabilitation should be balanced so that natives will continue insofar as practicable to produce their own foodstuffs while obtaining the benefits of wage income from these sources and, at the same time, developing means of greater self-sufficiency for current and later use.

12. *Savings and Savings Institutions*

Native savings should be encouraged and appropriate institutions for facilitating savings should be provided. The volume and type of goods now on island markets are insufficient to provide essential items for the native economy. Presumably these goods will become available. Natives should be encouraged to keep their surplus funds, if any, until such goods do appear in their markets. Difficulties of maintaining surplus funds for more valuable purposes at later dates will be reduced by providing depositories offering protection for their funds. The mechanics of operation may vary from area to area. In general, the main objective should be to provide safekeeping of individuals' funds in responsible hands.

Native experience and present conditions in the Marianas support a policy of encouraging and facilitating means for savings. There, natives are looking forward to imports of more goods, especially productive and durable goods, such as building materials, livestock, etc. Chamorros on Guam have a means for savings through the Bank of Guam. This service has been extended to Saipan on a periodic basis. Guamians have ready access to the institution. They can deposit or withdraw savings with comparative ease. This is an important feature of any savings institution serving the public, native or otherwise. Accessibility to deposits and withdrawals on Saipan is dependent upon the periodic visits of the bank's agents. Natives on Saipan, as well as other areas, previously had access to the Japanese postal-savings system which operated in each major area and island. Natives on Saipan and Palau also had access to local banks.

Native participation and responsibility should be encouraged in development of savings institutions. The degree to which natives can participate and the responsibility which they may assume will vary among regions and islands. The basic institutional framework and particular operational details should be a matter mostly of native responsibility. Outside participation and responsibility should be provided to the extent necessary for adequate organization and legal responsibility for safekeeping of funds. Natives' past experience should be used in establishing an institutional framework for savings. Saipan natives organized and operated a "Provident Fund" under the Germans and the "Chamorro Association" under the Japanese. These organizations offered a means for savings and also credit for their members. They were patterned along lines similar to credit unions which operate under federal and state statutes in the United States. These institutions provide savings and credit features of a coöperative bank. Local situations in the islands should be investigated with a view to determining if this type of approach offers feasible and economic means for handling native deposits. Organizations along these lines in the hands of natives should provide them with desirable financial services at a minimum of expense to the Administration. Cost of administration and details of accounting, and so forth, would be borne by the native members, thereby reducing outside participation to general responsibility for determining policy and operating principles.

In many areas a strongbox will provide sufficient means for safekeeping. This may be placed in appropriate hands, with native organizations attending to clerical details and assuming expenses of operation. In larger islands with relatively complex economy and greater populations, the depository should be sufficiently large to provide protection against known risks and to handle deposits and withdrawals with convenience. Again, accounting and operational details may be handled by natives, with administrative guidance. Surplus funds in the local depository may be periodically deposited, in the name of the native association, with outside depositories, such as the Bank of Guam.

Savings institutions should not be directly associated with trading enterprises. They may be combined with credit institutions, but not with other commercial activities. Safe depositories for natives' documents are just as desirable as savings institutions for funds. Their development should be considered coördinately with any consideration of savings.[3]

13. *Credit and Credit Institutions*

Credit policies should be adapted to essential needs of natives and should accord with their ability to use credit for promotion of their own welfare. Natives' experience with credit varies from area to area. People of the Marianas are relatively well acquainted with credit as a commercial institution. In other areas, natives' experience with credit is considerably more limited and in some areas largely absent. Natives in Palau have used credit in the past; limited forms of credit will serve a useful purpose again in that area. Past experience with credit in the Marshalls and in Ponape in general has not been satisfactory either in terms of the creditor or of the natives. However, some individuals, especially traders, deserve favorable consideration even in these areas.

Local situations should be analyzed to determine the feasibility and desirability of instituting credit arrangements in each given area.[4]

Liability for credit should be determined by the local pattern of responsibility. Liability may rest with the individual in the Marianas. In other areas, such as Palau and Yap, liability for credit to purchase items that benefit the community may lie with the community through the chiefs.

The following recommendations are offered with respect to credit policies for natives: (1) credit for current and continuing purchases of consumers' goods should be discouraged and limited; (2) consumer credit for productive purposes, such as purchases of durable goods, livestock, tools, and so forth, should be provided for natives in the Marianas and in Palau, and in some limited instances elsewhere; (3) commercial credit, that is, credit to finance imports, exports, and trading institutions, should be provided by outside sources to the extent that native savings are inadequate for financing such projects; (4) organizations of natives should be sponsored for the purpose of pooling native savings as a source of credit for their own members; (5) native production credit associations should be organized for the purpose of supplying credit to their members for specific productive purposes, such as increase in livestock numbers, increased plantings, or larger production; (6) a governmental medium should be established whereby local or regional native associations may obtain adequate financing to perform functions in the development and operation of approved, constructive programs; (7) adequate and specific advisory service should be provided through a continuing group to promote and guide the functions of governmental and native institutions in granting and using credit.

A need now exists in a number of areas for consumer-production credit by individuals and native organizations. Demand for credit will increase from these sources as more productive goods become available. The demand for consumer-production credit should be supplied by native organizations and individuals insofar as native financial resources permit. Where natives' aggregated savings are insufficient to meet credit demands, loans may be made to native credit organizations so that they in turn may deal directly with individuals or other elements in the native society which require credit.

The problem of determining an individual native's need for production credit is difficult if not impossible for an outsider. This judgment can be rendered best by his fellow natives. Also, his fellow natives can best determine the prospective borrower's responsibility and honesty. The development of native associations along credit-union lines may offer the most practical and feasible approach to operation of native credit facilities, while, at the same time, reducing the expense of operation by placing administrative details in the hands of the local organization.

Demand already exists for commercial credit by native trading institutions to help finance purchases of trade goods and sales of surplus products. The prospects are that demand for this type of credit will increase in accordance with the volume of imports and exports. Demand for commercial credit will in general exceed the capacity of local native institutions to supply it. Outside sources of credit are essential to supply the additional credit. Usual outside credit sources are not adequately equipped or uniquely experienced to handle satisfactorily the types of credit needs arising in such situations. The total volume of credit required within the foreseeable future in the area will, by mainland standards, be comparatively small. Prospects of a profitable operation are not bright. A quasi-governmental credit organization appears necessary. Administrative costs should be borne by the government. If possible, funds should be provided either from direct Federal sources, with sufficient latitude of operation to meet a variety of unique native credit requirements, or funds should be derived from recognized philanthropic institutions.

14. *Savings and Credit Institutions*

Institutions for promoting savings or providing credit may be combined wherever both needs exist. Among the more primitive groups, it seems probable that services at first will be limited mostly to promoting savings and establishing a depository. As economic needs develop among such groups, or as requirements may now exist, credit services may become a coördinate part of the savings and depository functions. In either instance, such institutions whether they operate entirely on a native basis or in combination with outside resources, will play a unique role in the local economy. Most probably, financial resources of the community and demands upon them will require that both savings and credit needs can best be served through the operation of a single institution within any given community. Such institutions will then assume a monopoly role in the community they serve. As such, they will bear a heavy responsibility which must be recognized in their operating policies if they are to serve the best interests of the community. Such an institution should not be required to perform its services for the entire community at a financial loss. Neither should its objective be to make huge profits. Instead, its role should be entirely that of a service institution, with equitable charges for services balanced against equitable returns to natives furnishing investment capital. Periodic reports should be furnished on any institution set up to meet these purposes. Its organization should be formalized through written charter or bylaws and licenses. The size of the organization should be determined largely by the size of the area and population which it serves. Ready accessibility to all natives should be one of its paramount features.

Additional organizations may be established along the same lines and for the same purpose within islands or other subdivisions of regions as ready accessibility and convenience necessitates. Coöperative banks patterned after credit unions should be encouraged to meet depository and credit requirements. They would offer an opportunity for natives to organize for their own benefit along financial lines. Basic cultural patterns upon which such organizations may rest exist in practically all areas. Such institutions would not only provide basic institutional foundations for deposits and credit levels but they also would help provide the organized channels through which natives may deal with outside financial institutions.

The Bank of Guam now provides depository services for natives of that island and for those of Saipan. It also offers a limited amount of credit. The bank's resources will allow it to expand its credit facilities considerably if the demand for credit increases and the bank's policies are shaped to meet such credit needs. Owing to the position the Bank of Guam holds within the island, it is in fact a monopoly. Because of this position and the volume of savings which natives have in the bank, it perforce bears a heavy responsibility for the welfare of Guam natives and its policies should be directed accordingly. Its credit policies will influence to a great extent the direction and speed of Guam's economic recovery and rehabilitation. As a direct operating agent of the Naval Government of Guam, it should perform not only depository and exchange services for Guam natives but it should also assist in the organization of business enterprise to serve essential needs of the island's residents. It is recommended that the Bank of Guam employ as one of its officers a qualified person whose main function would be to determine business needs and to help in organization of new business.

15. *Public Finance*

General over-all responsibility for financing public works and other expenditures in the general or public interest of natives should rest with a single agency. Types of expenditures may vary from those for education, health and sanitation, public safety, and general administration to construction of schools, dispensaries, hospitals, utilities, or payments for agricultural incentives, housing, or capital installations for economic enterprise. Presumably any such payment would be approved as a program of promoting native rehabilitation and welfare, but the sum total of the program should be coördinated and integrated as reasonably well balanced in the interest of native welfare. The relative importance of specific phases of the total program may change from area to area depending upon local conditions growing out of the extent of war damage or natives' previous standards of living. Coördination of planning and operation is essential in order to justify expenditures as well as in the ultimate interest of natives.

Major sources of funds must, of necessity, be other than native. Native resources are and will continue to be extremely limited until rehabilitation has progressed much further than it has at present. Previous administrations were obliged to depend primarily upon their home governments for financial support. Economic conditions in the islands today do not warrant any more optimistic outlook for self-support than they did in the past.

Public expenditure in the islands may be classified generally as (1) support of native welfare only, and (2) combinations of native and non-native welfare. Expenditures for native and non-native welfare should be made only out of Federal funds at the present time. Although natives may benefit from improved roads, more adequate and convenient water supplies, better docks, and so forth, they should not be required to finance these improvements if they are also constructed for the use of occupying forces. Expenditures for native welfare only may be in part from native sources; however, the ability of natives to support such expenditures should be considered in the light of their present economic status. Whenever native funds are expended they should be carefully explained to native authorities, and expenditures should be made only after the considered approval of native officials is obtained. Administrators bear not only a heavy responsibility in the handling of any public funds but also an added responsibility in the collection or expending of native funds. Natives resented the manner in which Japanese often handled native funds. Similar pitfalls may be avoided to some extent if a clear and comprehensive understanding is maintained at all times with natives in the assessment, collection, and expenditure of funds derived from local sources.

Federal funds must be relied upon to provide the main source of expenditures relating to native welfare and economic development during the period of rehabilitation and reconstruction. Expenditures for current operation, apart from administrative expenses, may be supported to some extent from native sources, although the ability of native economy to bear such expenses should be analyzed in the light of natives' current needs and their former economic status.

16. *Taxes*

It is part of the essence of good government for the governed to share at least partially in the responsibilities of government. No portion of that responsibility is more keenly felt than in the case of tax levies and collections. Under the best of circumstances, payment of taxes is usually an onerous duty and frequently a source of irritation. The tradition of the American people on this subject induces a cautionary note in any approach to a tax problem. Islanders do not appreciate "taxation without representation" any more than do Americans.

Any consideration of tax programs for islanders in the Marianas, Carolines, or Marshalls should be viewed in the light of current and foreseeable conditions. The chief problem now facing islanders is the all-important matter of satisfying their essential living requirements, which will take all the energies and financial resources they can command during the next several years. Owing to the ravages of combat, natives in Saipan, Rota, Yap, Palau, Truk, Ponape, Kusaie, and main centers in the Marshalls have had much, if not most, of their major economic resources nullified or destroyed; economic opportunities (except for Guam) are close to or even below bare subsistence levels; natives' savings are inaccessible, frozen, or lost; homes have been seriously damaged or, more commonly, completely obliterated; schools, hospitals, and other essential public facilities were bombed out of existence and present facilities are but temporary; land and property claims allowable under international law have not been settled; in general, the native economy in practically the entire area is in a serious state of maladjustment, with natives having no alternative but to direct most of their energies to providing bare subsistence considerably below prewar levels.

Because of these conditions, it is recommended that no new tax program should be instituted until specific analyses have been made of the extent of islanders' rehabilitation needs in terms of homes, productive industries, agriculture, and income-producing enterprises. Proposed revenue measures should be tied directly to specific appropriations for definite purposes. Approval of appropriations and of revenue measures should be based upon review and consent by islanders as well as by the Administration. Proposals for appropriations of native funds and for revenue measures should be presented to islanders through their duly constituted authorities in simple but specific terms, stating the alleged necessity for expenditures and levies, the purpose, amounts required, rates of levy, points of impost, method of collection, times of collection, and method of accounting; these terms should then be translated into the local vernacular and taken to the people by their representatives, with the request that a complete and accurate reflection of the islanders' reaction to the proposal shall be given to the Administration.

It is also recommended that *no labor levies or material levies* should be imposed. Experience in virtually every area where such forms of levies have been used offers abundant evidence of the serious difficulties in equitably applying such forms, as well as the probability of abuses growing out of their use.

After due consideration of economic and social conditions in an area, if it is deemed appropriate to institute procedure preliminary to a tax program in Micronesia (other than Guam), an annual tax on males of working age appears to be the most desirable for general imposition. Excise taxes on such items as tobacco, cosmetics, and so forth (but not on essentials), may be considered as a future possibility, as also income taxes. It is important that a thorough study be made of previous tax measures in specific areas, and the reaction of islanders to them, whenever any preliminary consideration is extended to revenue proposals. Consideration of tax programs in other Pacific Island dependencies would be useful.[5]

17. *Appropriation of Native Funds*

Control of the public purse strings is just as dear to the hearts of islanders as it is to any other group of individuals. Therefore, extreme caution should be exercised in the expenditure of funds derived from native sources. The amount of revenue which may be derived from local sources will of necessity constitute only a small proportion, as it has in the past, of the total cost of rehabilitating islanders or even of the total cost of current administration, even after restoration of the former economic status. The major responsibility must be borne by the Administration, as it has been by past administrations. The sense of responsibility for expenditure of public funds may be obtained by direct participation of the governed in the consideration of proposed expenditures. To this end, it is recommended that extended public hearings, or other appropriate forms of native participation, should be followed in determining appropriation measures as well as revenue measures. The Administration should exercise prudence, caution, and restraint in consideration of types of activities for which appropriation from native sources should be expended. It is recommended that revenues from native sources should not be used to help finance activities which support American military or civilian projects. There are more than a sufficiency of strictly native activities to absorb all possible native revenues. It is recommended that revenues from natives sources may be expended for:

1. Maintenance or partial maintenance of schools for natives, and payment or partial payment of salaries of schoolteachers and native medical practitioners;
2. Maintenance of water supply, general or local, for use of natives;
3. Drainage for sanitation or conservation used only by natives;
4. Sanitary facilities in general for native communities;

5. Local roads and bridges for native use only, not ordinarily necessary for or used by military forces;

6. Maintenance of small docks, moorings, and so forth, for sole use by groups of native seamen or traders;

7. Clearing of land for the location of any building or facility installed for the sole benefit of the native community.

Primary consideration should be given to the fact that a major governmental task confronting the present Administration in Micronesia is the rehabilitation of islanders' economy. The development of their previous economic levels resulted primarily from relatively large expenditures by outside sources. There appears to be no alternative to that course again, if islanders are to enjoy similar economic benefits under the present Administration. Therefore, local revenue measures and appropriations of funds from local sources should be viewed in a proper perspective, namely, as a means of inviting native participation in the responsibility for their own government rather than as a means for accomplishing the total task of rehabilitation and current administration.

C. PUBLIC FACILITIES

In planning for the rehabilitation of Micronesians, community needs may be easily slighted in the preoccupation with the more pressing individual needs of food, housing, and clothing. Public facilities should be given close attention for reasons of public health and safety, as well as in recognition of the need to rebuild community life itself. The Chamorros may constitute a notable exception to the generalization about community spirit, in view of the individualistic character which these people have acquired through centuries of contact with western civilization, and yet for this very reason public facilities have come to play a more important part in their lives than elsewhere in the islands.

Prior to the war, most Micronesians did not enjoy the use of many public facilities, but wherever facilities existed they were greatly appreciated by the natives and came to be integral parts of their culture. Public utilities and services, such as water supply, sewage disposal, electricity, schools, hospitals and dispensaries, churches, government offices, and parks and playgrounds, were developed in proportion to the association with foreign communities.

Native water supplies for drinking were derived mainly from rainwater catchment and storage in cisterns and tanks, while water for bathing and washing was drawn from brackish wells, springs, and streams. Water was piped into towns on Guam and Saipan and in Palau; a few native homes tapped this source, but most town dwellers drew their water from community outlets constructed at intervals along the main pipeline. Near Ponape (Colony), a dam was built across the Tawenjokola River to create a reservoir for public use. The Japanese government generally subsidized the construction of native public baths and washing places.

About the only concessions to modern sanitation in the matter of sewage disposal were pit latrines and a few septic tanks. Flush toilets were built indoors in the better homes in Agaña and Garapan. Once more, the Japanese government offered subsidies to those who built proper latrines, in an effort to wean the natives away from the aboriginal custom of utilizing the outer shore and high tide to dispose of excreta.

As early as the twenties, electric lighting was available for limited use in Garapan, Koror, Angaur, Yap (Town), Dublon, Ponape (Colony), Lele, and Jabor - about one light bulb for each house, at nominal cost. The Japanese government operated small generators with diesel or gasoline engines to provide, not only electric light, but power for wireless and other facilities. The dam near Ponape (Colony) was intended to supply water power for a hydroelectric plant at Nanpil. Chamorros on Guam owned and operated a power plant which supplied electricity to a number of native homes in Agaña. Elsewhere in the islands, kerosene lamps were the primary source of domestic lighting.

In each district capital, public buildings, such as churches, schools, hospitals, government offices, wireless stations, and meteorological posts, were well constructed of wood or concrete and had iron roofing. In addition, at Koror, there were solid structures to house the Tropical Industries Research Institute (with branches at Saipan and Ponape), the Marine Products Experiment Station, and the Products Museum. Leprosariums were located at Saipan, Palau, Yap, and other district centers, and government hospitals were equipped with laboratory facilities, X-ray equipment, and operating rooms, as well as wards for native patients. The town of Agaña was distinguished by similar public structures in concrete, including the buildings of the Guamian Congress. Trade stores, of which there were usually several in competition in each large community, were sturdily built, wooden, frame structures with iron roofs, plenty of shelf space, and storage room in back.

Particularly in the central and western Carolines, each native settlement possessed a men's clubhouse, elaborately decorated structures which were built along native styles and were considerably larger than any private dwelling; these buildings occupied an essential place in the community life of the people. On Dublon, several wooden shelters existed for the use of visiting natives from other islands. Elsewhere, community assembly halls, built of thatch and native timbers or of wood siding and iron roofing, afforded space for council meetings and other public gatherings.

The larger towns on Guam and Saipan and in the Carolines had beautiful parks, with ornamental trees and rocks, swings for children, and pavilions for musical concerts and public oratory. Recreation fields, equipped with playground facilities, and baseball diamonds were a part of every government school unit.

Wherever public facilities had been developed in connection with government or military installations, the war took a heavy toll and reduced their benefits to the native population to almost nothing. Public buildings were destroyed or badly damaged by bomb and shellfire; their concrete skeletons are a familiar sight today as they rear bleakly above the desolation of leveled settlements. Power plants were gutted or have deteriorated from exposure. Waterworks are in such bad shape that public health is menaced.

Buildings are gradually being replaced as natives erect thatched structures for temporary use until more permanent building materials can be obtained. Opensided native shelters large enough to accommodate large gatherings are being used for school classes, church services, and council meetings. The Administration has erected Quonset huts and wooden frame buildings from military stockpiles to establish hospital and other essential services.[1]

Electric lighting facilities are available in those few areas where natives have been able to avail themselves of power generated primarily for military purposes. In Saipan, families in large towns are allotted one light bulb in each house; elsewhere, electricity is used in a few communities for limited public facilities. Where home lighting had been customary before the war, natives now lack generators, fuel, and light bulbs to restore these benefits. The natives want electricity again and are willing to pay for it as they did before, but at present most of them have had to return to the use of kerosene lanterns.[2]

Water supply is a more serious concern. Cisterns have cracked and fallen apart, wells have become clogged with debris through lack of maintenance when populations were dislocated during the war, and outside water lines have been severed or dismantled. Inspection of present sources of drinking water reveals a potential danger to public health. Natives cry for cement to rebuild their cisterns and wells, for iron roofing to catch rainwater, and for piping to reëstablish the water systems of former years.

Sewage-disposal methods have retrogressed in many areas to the aboriginal practice of defecating on the outer shores and letting the tide do the rest. Where public latrines have been constructed for large settlements, as at Chalan Canoa on Saipan, they are too few in number. In Palau, trucks are badly needed to haul away the accumulated sewage. While the natives of Yap for years resisted the efforts of the Japanese government to install adequate water and sewage facilities, they stand ready under American administration to begin such construction as soon as supplies can be provided.

Stores and other structures necessary in the economy of native communities are inadequate. In many places, the Administration has had former *Nanyo Boeki Kaisha* store buildings repaired; elsewhere, thatched structures have been erected to house the trading activities of the community. Copra sheds, warehouses, and boathouses used by the community are in need of repair and are too few in number for any increase in economic activity.

Where health is endangered by the lack of public facilities, the restoration of those facilities should receive the same priority as food, housing, and transportation; other public facilities may be regarded as secondary needs.

The Administration should assume the obligation of restoring public utilities and services for natives, such as schools, hospitals and dispensaries, water supply, sewage disposal, and council buildings; their maintenance might be provided through tax levies on the population when an economic balance has been regained in the locality. It is assumed that all churches and other mission properties will be restored at the expense of the mission societies operating in the islands, any claims for damages incurred during the war being presented to authorities at the proper time.

High priority should be attached to the procurement of building supplies - cement, lumber, iron roofing, piping - and tools for reconstruction of community structures and water and sewage facilities. Inventories of military stockpiles in the islands should be canvassed for possible fulfillment of these requirements. Abandoned military installations, both Japanese and American, should be dismantled to provide salvage materials for distribution to native communities according to need.

Subsidies should be offered to natives by the Administration to encourage the building of latrines and septic tanks for more efficient disposal of sewage, the construction of cisterns and rainwater-catchment apparatus for more sanitary storage of water supplies, and the erection of community structures which are essential to the native economy, such as copra sheds, warehouses, and boathouses.

Natives should be directed as an emergency measure to use a single community building for various public assemblies; for example, a single structure could be used as school, church, assembly hall, and recreation center. Playground equipment for school children should be provided, and baseball diamonds and other athletic facilities created for community use.

Electricity for lighting and power should be provided for native use wherever the opportunity exists. Small amounts of electricity could be diverted at a nominal charge from power plants installed for military use. In other cases, natives should be provided with generators, fuel, wiring, and light bulbs to restore and expand the facilities which they had before the war. This should be done on the principle of inexpensive and simple equipment designed for low-cost operation compatible with the natives' limited income.

D. TRANSPORTATION[1]

Of necessity, transportation must be a foundation on which to base any economic program for Micronesian peoples. Without transport facilities, as demonstrated this past year, trade goods cannot be distributed, copra and other native produce cannot be collected for export, the normal economic activities of the native community are seriously disrupted, and regular administrative services cannot be provided. The solution to the transportation problem will provide part answer to other rehabilitation problems which face the islanders today - distribution of food, clothing, and building supplies, allocation of labor resources, and resettlement of displaced persons and communities.

As might be expected in an insular region, development of land transport in Micronesia, especially as regards the use of vehicles by natives, has been only nominal. Trails, pathways, and narrow streets serve communities, and relatively good networks of roads on such high islands as Guam, Saipan, and Yap connect some villages and towns with one another. However, just prior to the war, only 340 miles of road were reported for the entire mandated area, of which 147 miles were less than 12 feet in width, and only 24 miles were more than 21 feet wide. In most islands, coastwise shipping has been less difficult to maintain than roads. Railroads for the accommodation of passengers did not exist. A few bus systems were being operated on a limited scale on Guam and Saipan. Automobiles were owned almost entirely by non-natives. Natives depended on foot, bicycle, and cart to move about or carry burdens. In Guam, the bullcart was commonplace, while everywhere else in Micronesia the bicycle was more popular owing to Japanese influence. (See Table VIII.)

TABLE VIII. VEHICLES OWNED BY JAPANESE AND NATIVES BY ADMINISTRATIVE DISTRICT, 1937

Vehicles	Saipan	Palau	Yap	Truk	Ponape	Jaluit	Total
Bicycles	9,351	2,270	131	416	514	346	13,028
Carts and Wagons	3,242	71	14	24	7	115	3,473
Automobiles	159	30	1	7	7	1	205
Total	12,752	2,371	146	447	528	462	16,706

Palau was the hub of a Japanese commercial airplane network, planes connecting with Yap, Tinian, Saipan, Truk, Ponape, and Jaluit, with Japan and Formosa, and with Portuguese Timor; natives made almost no use of these services.

The islanders once had a notable reputation for competent seamanship and made long voyages in their sailing canoes, but Germans and Japanese discouraged canoe traffic on the high seas for various reasons. The Japanese permitted, and encouraged, natives to travel on regular trading vessels, as deck passengers at scheduled fares and providing their own food and sleeping gear. Each year thousands of Micronesians availed themselves of this service and journeyed from one island to another to visit friends and relatives or to trade at the district capitals. In recent years 10 per cent of interisland travelers in the Marianas and nearly 40 per cent in the Palaus were natives. Such trips were generally restricted to vessels operating within a single administrative district. However, each year a few selected natives were sent to Japan at government expense, and others made infrequent trips to British and French colonies south of the equator.

Offshore operations of native craft were limited generally to the sheltered waters inside the reefs or to deep-sea fishing not far from land. In the western islands, native skills in navigation and seamanship have become a lost art; only in the Marshalls and in the central Carolines do the natives seem to retain to any degree the sailing traditions of former years. Sail and power craft registered for commercial fishing were in the hands of non-natives in most cases. Activities of the latter were most extensive in the Palaus, least in the Marshalls and in Guam.

TABLE IX. VESSELS USED IN COMMERCIAL FISHING BY ADMINISTRATIVE DISTRICT, 1937

Fishing Crafts	Saipan	Palau	Yap	Truk	Ponape	Total
Less than 5 tons, no power	89	80	7	100	51	227
Less than 20 tons, powered	36	58	-	52	14	160
More than 20 tons, powered	4	146	-	4	1	154
Total	129	284	7	156	66	541

Each port in the islands was served by a small number of harbor craft - barges, tugs, lighters, sampans, launches - most of them equipped with diesel engines. These craft were usually owned and operated by Japanese and Okinawans, except where natives in the western Carolines managed several fleets of interisland ferries.

Under the Japanese, shipping services which had been instituted by the Germans were considerably expanded. In 1922, the South Seas Bureau arranged with *Nippon Yusen Kaisha* (NYK - Japan Mail Steamship Company) to maintain regular steamer service between Japan and the principal islands of the mandated area, and with *Nanyo Boeki Kaisha* (NBK - South Seas Trading Company) to do the same between the main islands and adjacent isles. Subsidies from the government for these operations averaged ¥700,000 annually, five-sixths of that amount going to *Nippon Yusen Kaisha*.

Before the war, NYK operated four steamship lines between Japan and the Mandated Islands. The Saipan Line served only the Marianas, the Western Line contacted Palau and Yap en route to the Philippines and the East Indies, the Eastern Line served the eastern Carolines and the Marshalls via Saipan, and the East-West Line tied Palau to Truk, Ponape, and Jaluit. Saipan and Tinian were in most frequent contact with Japan, Palau next, Jaluit and Rota trailing last; most district capitals were visited by NYK steamers about five times a month. NYK and NBK schedules combined to provide regular service from the mandated area, not only to Japan, but also to the Philippines, the East Indies, New Guinea, New Caledonia, Fiji, and the Gilbert Islands.

For the most part, interisland trading within the mandated area was maintained by NBK sailing vessels equipped with auxiliary engines. Five regular lines operated to serve the outlying islands with regular freight and passenger service, although the frequency of trips varied from four times a week to three times a year depending on the commercial importance of the areas concerned. Trading runs began at Saipan, Yap, Palau, Truk, Ponape, and Jaluit. After 1937, a private concern in the Marianas operated a sailing vessel between Saipan and Guam several times a year.

Just as food resources and housing throughout the islands were damaged or destroyed by the ravages of war, so were transportation facilities drastically reduced. Many vehicles of all kinds were rendered useless by explosives, others have rusted and deteriorated beyond repair, and only a few can be restored to service by replacement of essential parts. Hundreds of vessels were burned or scuttled by strafing and sabotage, and the hulks lie on their side in shallow waters, rusting and rotting because there are no materials with which to recondition them. Roads are in bad shape, bridges are reduced to rubble, concrete and wood piers are pitted and burned from bomb and shellfire, and canals are still blocked by debris. Resources to rehabilitate these facilities are practically nonexistent in most of the islands, and outside assistance in no small measure is needed to achieve some semblance of prewar conditions.

Military operations, particularly on Guam and in the Marianas, have provided access to all parts of some larger islands by means of relatively well-built and durable roads. The maintenance of these roads and the restoration of highway facilities in nonmilitary areas is currently carried on by American service personnel with modern road equipment, except in a few islands where Military Government has drafted available native labor to do the same work, a procedure reminiscent of the labor tax imposed by preceding administrations. Such diversion of native manpower has interfered seriously with more vital projects in the natives' own communities, such as restoration of housing and cultivation of food crops. Many miles of roadway once required for military operations will not be needed in peacetime and are already being abandoned.

A public bus system has been restored on Guam under Navy organization and management; although some equipment has been procured from surplus military stocks on the island, more busses and heavy-duty trucks are needed. On Saipan and other military bases, some natives are dissatisfied with Military Government practice of requiring laborers to be transported in trucks at arbitrary hours to their place of employment. Other natives, without any means of public transport, often find it necessary to walk long distances to trading stores and to hospital dispensaries.[2]

Private transport facilities on land are just as inadequate. There is a great need for bicycles, light pushcarts, and bullcarts, or at least for parts and materials to recondition the vehicles which survived the war. Wheels, tires, and axles are in greatest demand, and draft animals are not in sufficient number to satisfy transport needs. Where the Administration has distributed worn-out jeeps and Japanese trucks among the local population, the natives face problems of fuel supply and repair; generally, the people lack the training for proper care and operation of automotive equipment, and the expense involved is out of the question for the average native purse.

The current water transportation picture has two aspects: one is that of primary supply lines between the islands and Guam or other main ports located outside of the mandated area; the other is that of small boat traffic within the various island areas. The present service between Guam or Honolulu and distribution points, such as Kwajalein, Ponape, Truk, Yap, and others, is neither regular nor is it adequate. There is no provision for native passengers between island capitals, except in unusual instances. Kusaie and Yap, in particular, do not receive any supplies for months at a time, and there is bitter disappointment to islanders when naval vessels put into port on some special mission but with little or no supplies; this is largely due to poor coördination between supply authorities and port directors at the vessels' point of origin. Irregular schedules have cost the Administration a good deal of prestige and have resulted in considerable anxiety and suffering for natives, who have no idea how long they must ration their limited supplies. At present, the distribution of trade goods and collection of native products by water depend primarily upon the logistic requirements of the military, the needs of islanders being of secondary concern.

The restoration of small boat facilities for fishing and interisland transport has been left pretty much to native ingenuity and resourcefulness. In Palau, the islanders are reviving a prewar coöperative venture in ferrying freight and passengers between the islands of that area, but their vessels are few and decrepit, and their funds which were held in trust by the Japanese administration are now frozen with all other yen assets. In some cases, the Administration has begun to procure surplus whaleboats and buoy tenders for the use of natives, who fit them with sail or equip them with engines for atoll use, but this program has barely started and is confined mostly to the Marshalls. Generally, the natives are reconditioning the few Japanese vessels which were not completely destroyed and are slowly building up a fleet of canoes and small sailboats. Most activity with sail has been carried on in the eastern islands, centering in the Marshalls where the industry of the natives is particularly encouraging despite the dire need of sailcloth, rope, and hardware, not to mention tools. Elsewhere in the islands, sail is often considered a backward step by natives who have grown accustomed to depend on power in their water craft.

The number of Japanese power boats which the natives have been able to put back into service is not many, nor are they adequate to existing transport requirements. The difficulties facing natives in this task are varied: lumber is scarce for replacement of rotted or splintered planks in boat hulls; there is little rope or marine hardware available; but the principal problem is power propulsion. Japanese engines are low-power, burn a very heavy diesel oil, and cost little to operate. Supplies of Japanese diesel fuel are dangerously low in the islands, and experiments in the substitution of American fuel in Japanese engines have not been successful. So that American oil stocks in the islands might be turned to advantage for native use, a few marine engines of American manufacture have been installed in native boats, but American engines are too high-powered, too complicated to keep in repair, and too expensive for natives to operate. Natives lack both training in motor mechanics and facilities of machine shops for proper care and maintenance of American engines. The power units of reconditioned Japanese craft are held together today with pieces of rope and baling wire; to go beyond the reef in such dilapidated craft is dangerous and has already resulted in serious accidents. In this regard, there is a need for navigational aids for native boat operators; at present they leave port entirely on their own responsibility with no radio contact or other communication in case of trouble. This has resulted in the practical restriction of most native water operations to sheltered waters within lagoon or reef. (In Yap, the repair of the Tagaren Canal has provided safe passage between the northern and southern islands.)

Many village and atoll communities have expressed a desire to buy or acquire in some way new boats for their local use. Where this has been carried out, ownership and operation of the craft rest in the hands of district chiefs, or councils, or private entrepreneurs, depending on the local customs.

Native inhabitants of the islands should be guaranteed freedom of movement as passengers at scheduled fares on regular transportation facilities provided by the Administration, by native enterprise, or by any other transport concern, both within Micronesia and between the islands and other areas in the Pacific basin. In this connection, the Administration should facilitate the procedure by which natives may obtain permission to travel from Guam and the former mandated area to other United States territories and to areas controlled by other nations.

Transportation between Micronesia and outside areas should be adequate to provide sufficient and constant flow of supplies to the native population at readily accessible points of distribution, and to provide export outlets for native produce. Where American or foreign business firms are interested in operating vessels between Micronesia and other areas in the Pacific basin, or between such central points within the islands as Guam, Saipan, Palau, Yap, Truk, Ponape, Kusaie, and Kwajalein or Majuro, the Administration should raise no obstacle other than to prevent the development of exploitation or of any private monopoly.

Adequate transportation facilities should be reëstablished immediately within the islands, both in terms of direct provision by the Administration as well as indirectly through native supplementation. Adequacy should be measured by the frequency and volume of service enjoyed by the natives under the Japanese.

Regularity of transport schedules should be emphasized in providing freight and passenger service to every populated atoll and island. Monthly service should be the general standard, with more frequent schedules where the local traffic demands. As an emergency measure, until more regular and frequent schedules are established, the agency in charge of distribution of trade goods and supplies should coördinate its work with that of port directors in order to make every possible use of naval vessels leaving Guam and other supply bases for outlying islands, regardless of the vessels' primary mission.

Schedules of passenger and freight rates for transport services in the islands should be established equitably with due regard for the average native income prevailing in each area. In order to protect natives from unduly heavy costs, rate schedules should be closely scrutinized from time to time. Where shipping which is operated by the Administration or by private enterprise offers competition to native-controlled shipping, care should be exercised not to undercut native tariffs. When non-natives, especially administrative officials, travel on native craft, they should pay the established rate for such service. If several classes of passenger rates are maintained on larger vessels, the facilities provided for native passengers should be inspected periodically by administrative officials for adherence to the principles of sanitation and human welfare.

The Administration should construct or maintain public thoroughfares and navigational aids wherever the traffic demands. Where principal use of these facilities is made by administrative agencies, the cost of maintenance should be borne by the Administration; where the traffic is entirely native, a tax might be devised as soon as the native economy seems able to bear it. Where navigational aids, such as radio communication, markers, and air-sea rescue facilities, are not available for the safety of natives operating their craft beyond the reefs, every effort should be made to establish such aid rather than to restrict native operations on the excuse of a lack of safety precautions.

In the maintenance of roads, the Administration should use modern road equipment and employ a small force of trained natives, in place of intermittent hiring of large numbers of unskilled laborers drawn from the normal activities of the native community. It is recommended that natives be used as full-time workers wherever possible in the operation and maintenance of traffic facilities; they should be given proper training and be paid wages commensurate with the duties which they perform.

The training of natives in ship carpentry, motor mechanics, radio communication, operation of road-repair equipment, navigation, weather observation, and related skills should be made an integral part of any native educational program in order to provide qualified personnel for the operation of land and water transport facilities, either as civil service employees or in the execution of natives' own enterprises.

A high priority should be applied to the procurement and distribution of essential items and materials for use in the rehabilitation of native transportation facilities. An inventory should be made of salvageable and surplus stores still available in stockpiles of war material remaining in the islands; items which are needed by natives should be distributed on a reasonable basis to local populations. Heavy trucks and busses are needed for public transport systems in Guam and Saipan; jeep wheels and axles can be adapted to bullcarts in the same area; small boats, such as buoy tenders and whaleboats, can be rigged for atoll use; fuel supplies are in great demand but must be adapted to Japanese engines in many instances; lumber, canvas, rope, and marine hardware are sorely needed for reconditioning craft of all kinds; tools are not adequate for the job of reconstruction; machine-shop equipment is desirable for local repairs of engines; and engines are needed for native-operated craft, particularly in Palau. Whether such equipment is given to the natives outright, at a nominal cost, or on some long-term loan, title to the property should be clearly understood by both parties; in general, it is desirable to establish title with the native – with district chiefs, atoll councils, or private entrepreneurs, depending on the local situation.

Attention should be given to the introduction of draft animals – carabao and cattle – in those islands where there is need for them.

The possibility of securing from Japan certain transportation equipment, such as fishing sampans, bicycles, and light two-wheeled pushcarts, should be investigated.

Expert investigation should be made of the possibilities of adapting Japanese low-power engines so that American diesel fuel can be used in them, in order to make use of available engine resources now in the hands of the natives. If such conversion is not successful, a source of similar low-power engines should be sought outside the islands to provide natives with motive power at a lower cost of operation than is possible with the average American marine engine.

Encouragement and practical aid, including subsidy, should be given to the development of native-controlled and native-operated transport enterprises, such as bus systems in towns or on larger islands, the ferryboat *kumiai* which is being revived in Palau, and small-boat construction projects, both to augment the islands' transportation facilities and to add to the income of the native population. The contribution of native resources should be integrated with the Administration's program to the utmost that local conditions and developments permit.

Where extra space is available in planes making regular flights between islands, it is recommended that natives be permitted to travel by air for legitimate purposes upon certification by an administrative officer, as in the case of travel to central schools, hospitals, places of employment, or for cases of personal emergency.

Investigation should be made of the possibilities in terms of time and personnel savings by the increased use of air transport by administrative and medical officers inspecting native populations. Such air travel might be profitably tied in with air-sea rescue operations within the area and integrated with an island's communication system for ready provision of emergency relief to outlying islands and atolls.

E. COMMUNICATION

Americans stationed in the islands express amazement at the rapidity with which news travels among the native population. Word-of-mouth communication has been, and probably will continue to be, the principal means of news dissemination for the islanders. Rumors and gossip spread whenever a native travels from one place to another; the total volume of news is in direct proportion to the number of transients. Personal messages, letters, and even packages, are carried willingly by native travelers for their friends who stay behind. Patients arrive at the hospitals from outlying islands, native laborers are drawn from many islands for the camps at military bases, and native interpreters accompany Administration parties on their rounds of the islands – all of them providing considerable opportunity for the rapid exchange of information from other areas.

In Japanese times other mediums of communication were available to natives, but rare use was made of them except in the case of postal service, by means of which natives in distant islands could correspond and even order goods from mail-order houses in Japan and the United States. Post offices were established at Saipan (Garapan), Tinian, Yap, Palau (Koror and Angaur), Truk (Dublon), Ponape (Colony), and Jaluit (Jabor); special post office branches were set up at Rota, Fais, and Kusaie. All were staffed by Japanese postmasters and clerks, their activities being coördinated under the postmaster at Garapan. These post offices served adjacent islands and operated under similar regulations as governed postal matters in Japan proper. Business handled at the post offices included ordinary mail, parcel post, postal money orders, postal savings, and telegrams. Mail was carried by NBK and NYK vessels when they made their trips through the islands of the mandated area and to Japan and other areas in the Pacific basin.

Telegrams were accepted in Japanese and in any European language. Wireless communication existed between the main islands, clearing through Palau to Japan. At Yap, connection was made by cable to Japan. Rates for interisland messages were lower than for those between the islands and Japan. Except for limited public telephone systems at Garapan and in the Palau Islands, telephone communications were restricted to government and military use. Some radio stations were established on main islands, but owing to practical difficulties few natives owned receiving sets.

Over a dozen newspapers were reported to have been published in the mandated area, in Japanese, but most of them were inconsequential. An official gazette was issued after 1936, containing changes in regulations for the notice of local officials throughout the islands. An excellent paper was printed by Palauans at Koror. Some natives subscribed to Japanese, German, and English newspapers and periodicals published outside the mandated area, receiving them regularly by mail through Japan. Except for occasional moving pictures of an educational nature, natives had no access to motion-picture entertainment.

On Guam, prior to the war, communications were not very different from those in the Japanese Mandate, except that regular United States mail service was in operation, and the natives enjoyed limited telephone facilities. Otherwise, as concerns the native population, the same general lack of radio, telegraph, and news mediums applied.

Under the American Administration at the present time, the only medium of communication available to natives is an irregular postal service operated by naval personnel. It is common for mail to arrive rather quickly at the proper FPO address of a Military Government unit and then be delayed for several months before delivery to natives in outlying islands and atolls; much of this confusion and delay results from lack of shipping. On Guam, where the Post Office Department continues to operate as in prewar times, the situation is better. Telephone facilities throughout the islands are for the sole use of military and government personnel.

Little is available in the way of newspapers for native reading. On Guam, *Navy News* is issued for service personnel at bases everywhere in Micronesia, but it is of small value to natives who cannot read English; those on Guam and Saipan who can read English are reported to enjoy it. For a time, Military Government at Kwajalein published a *News*

Review in English and Marshallese, a monthly digest of United States and world news and interesting local items of native import. It was well received by the Marshallese, but publication ceased in February 1946 because of lack of facilities and personnel. Some islanders are receiving issues of newspapers published in Honolulu and in the States. In the early days of American occupation of the islands, naval personnel visiting native settlements donated many back numbers of American news magazines, which were read from cover to cover by natives with a knowledge of English. This source of information about the outside world has dropped to almost nothing owing to this year's shipping shortage.[1]

Natives at military bases may attend moving pictures at nightly showings for service personnel. On occasion, naval vessels touring the islands are equipped with 16-millimeter projectors and have presented programs on shore for native enjoyment. Since few natives understand English well enough to follow the dialogue, their favorite movies are musicals and westerns.

Adequate facilities for handling ordinary mail, parcel post, and postal money orders should immediately be made available to islanders. At least monthly pickup and delivery should be guaranteed. It is recommended that native mail be processed as a collateral duty by a native interpreter on the staff of each Administration unit; he should be responsible for the collection of mailable matter at each atoll or island and for the distribution of whatever mail comes into his care. Mail destined for other near-by islands can be handled on an informal basis without entering the regular postal system, but mail going outside the district should be properly addressed and stamped for inclusion in the United States mail system. The native scribe in each locality should be designated as a local postmaster and be held responsible for the collection and distribution of postal matter within his immediate jurisdiction.

Telephone communication should be revived for public use in those areas like Guam and Saipan which had that service prior to the war, and wherever the public advantage can be usefully served. As an emergency service, it is recommended that telegraph and cable facilities maintained for government or military use be made available to natives with the approval of local administrative officials.

For practical reasons, radio reception by individual natives will remain nominal for some time. However, in the interest of public health and safety and for personal security in emergencies, as well as for possible utility in weather reporting for the military, it is recommended that a network of low-power radio stations be established in the islands. Not all atolls or islands would require this service immediately, and a judicial location of stations would insure a minimum of small boat travel from isolated places in case of emergencies. Eventually it would seem desirable to establish such communication posts for every outlying area. The cost of installation of radio equipment should be borne by the Administration as a public safety measure and as a navigational aid, if used in connection with weather observation. Equipment can be powered by gasoline generators or by storage batteries regularly charged by means of inexpensive wind charges; this system has been used with considerable success in the Canadian Arctic by the Hudson's Bay Company for trading purposes and for the personal security of its employees who are often isolated by weather conditions for months at a time. The maintenance and operation of radio stations should be handled by a corps of natives, adequately trained in radio techniques and weather observation, and employed as civil service personnel. This network should be integrated with the air-sea rescue system at present operative in the islands, and with whatever air transport facilities may be at the disposal of the Administration, to insure immediate relief for personal emergencies or public catastrophes reported from outlying islands and atolls.

As a further medium of communication, the Administration should be responsible for publication of bilingual newspapers for periodic distribution in the various linguistic areas of Micronesia, to help overcome the hiatus between news events in the islands and knowledge of them on the part of natives. The periodicals should be written and edited by natives for the island population, in both English and the local vernacular, with news of local interest, world news, educational features, and official notices. The cost of publication should be borne by the Administration as an educational measure. In those areas where an independent newspaper could feasibly be controlled and operated by natives, administrative encouragement should be provided; in Palau, where the natives have the experience to manage an independent newspaper, a small printing press and supplies are needed.

Back numbers of American news magazines and newspapers should be collected from the reading rooms and libraries serving American service personnel in the islands and be distributed to natives who can read English. Something in the way of a lending library should be considered as another means of placing news materials in the hands of news-hungry islanders.

F. CONSERVATION

1. *Human Resources*

In a broad sense, this whole report might be subtitled "How to Conserve the Human Resources of Micronesia," for every section concerns itself either directly or indirectly with this problem. It goes without saying that there is general acceptance of the ethical doctrine that Micronesians have a right to survival. But even leaving ethics aside, there are scientific grounds for desiring the conservation of human resources in Micronesia. These natives constitute a portion of the general reservoir of human variability. The future adaptability and improvement of the human species are dependent upon maintenance of a high degree of variability, and no one can rule out the possibility that Micronesians may possess traits of ultimate value for all mankind. For these as well as for the equally important ethical reasons, the Administration must guide its conduct of Micronesian affairs so as to conserve native human resources together with all natural resources which may now or eventually be useful to the natives. This consideration points up the urgent need for campaigns to reverse the downward population trends of Yap and other areas. It also adds weight to demands for health improvement programs and for cessation of the wasteful use of native labor. By the same token, natural resources must be scrupulously conserved: they are so very limited and dependence upon them is now or will become very close.

2. *Natural Resources*

Some valuable natural resources, such as phosphate and soils, are irreplaceable and consequently must be particularly zealously guarded. Others, such as forests and fish, are replaceable but require systematic maintenance. Because a certain resource has no apparent present value constitutes no reason that it may not some day prove valuable to local natives. Also, administrative officials must not, through preoccupation with needs of the present and immediate future, neglect the long-range need for conservation. There follow a few paragraphs on those natural resources which require special attention.

The importance to local economy of conserving phosphate resources for eventual use by Micronesians has already been stressed (Chapter III, Section H).

a. Soil. Above all, a program is required for preserving soil and soil fertility. Soil should be retained and enriched by suiting the type of land use to the topography and climate, by retaining rather than burning the vegetable debris, by maintaining watershed cover of forest on the steep areas of great rainfall, by maintaining vegetation (but not weeds) on land not actually under cultivation, by planting legumes for nitrogen fixation, by regulating grazing, and so forth. Such a program requires active participation of farmers and landholders.

A number of places in the Marianas, in Palau, and on Yap are suffering from soil erosion, initiated mainly by fire or by injudicious cultivation; erosion can and does occur on soils developed on both volcanic and limestone materials. Soil fertility is difficult to maintain under cultivation in tropical areas; high temperatures, heavy rainfall, and excessive cropping bring about leaching and loss of humus.

b. Water is an absolute necessity for human occupation of the Micronesian islands, but each kind of island presents a different conservation problem.

On the low islands it is a question of capturing and storing rain water; ground water is almost entirely lacking, or unfit for use, and cannot be significantly increased by conservation methods. Conservation of rain water concerns itself with constructing large and sanitary cisterns along with catchment areas, like roofs. In one sense, the water supply - for drinking purposes - can also be conserved by increasing the supply of coconut palms, for immature nuts provide potable liquid in a most satisfactory form.

On the high islands, rainfall, if properly utilized, is usually sufficient for all needs of the native populations. Mountainous watersheds should be protected as water reserves and their forest covers maintained, if adequate, or encouraged to recover, if destroyed. Human activities frequently impede forest recovery and have to be strictly controlled. Grazing has to be closely supervised, for otherwise it may bring on erosion in volcanic soils, or it may impede drainage of limestone soils by causing clogging of the pores. Well-drilling, pumping, and similar developments must be supervised by expert hydraulic engineers so that ground-water bodies will not be depleted or become saline. Large-scale pollution should be prevented at all costs. Hydroelectric power developments must be planned in such a way that they supplement water conservation activities.

c. Native plants and animals. Conservation of vegetation is also desirable for direct economic reasons. For the present, conservation dictates importation of lumber for emergency reconstruction; it is believed, however, that the islands eventually will be capable of supplying most of their local needs for lumber and other construction materials, as well as for handicraft, boat manufacture, and so forth, provided a proper forestry program is carried out. Supervision of this program should be in the hands of foresters with conservation backgrounds.

Conservation of vegetation is also desirable for important, but less apparent, indirect economic reasons. Micronesian islands contain many plants unknown elsewhere; some of them eventually may prove useful to Micronesia or to the world at large. (This applies also to the animal life inhabiting the vegetation; for example, certain harmless insects may be discovered as serving to control pests.)

The tropical ecology of Micronesia, a subject still in its infancy, will almost surely produce valuable information on how best to adapt these limited areas to the needs of a population hopefully expected to increase. Among other things, reserves of relatively undisturbed vegetation will provide reference points for gauging soil and vegetation changes taking place in regions subjected to human activities.

d. Future conservation programs. It is hoped and expected that Micronesians themselves will some day be prepared to plan and administer their own programs of conservation and industrial development. This will require foresters, soil scientists, entomologists, botanists, and so forth; therefore, natural reserves should be maintained for the edification of these future scientists, and these reserves should be located in the areas where they are to train and work.

Potential natural reserves include undisturbed forested areas on Rota, Saipan, Aguijan, northern Guam, the northern Marianas, western Babelthuap and the lowlands along the Garamiscan River, and on the limestone islands located between Koror and Peleliu. In addition, most areas above 200 meters altitude in the Carolines constitute fine potential reserves. None of the areas enumerated has much value as potential agricultural land.

3. *Economic Plants*

Important, also, is provision for preservation of stocks of the numerous varieties of local economic plants. Such plants as the breadfruit, banana, pandanus, the various taro-like plants, yams, coconuts, sweet potatoes, citrus, etc., have many variations. A great part of these are found only on one or a few islands. There is now a tendency to abandon the cultivation of many of these, because of the novelty of others introduced from abroad, and because of the general disturbance and dislocation of the native cultures resulting from the war and introduction of a foreign culture. However, any plant-breeding program involving established economic plants must depend for its raw materials on these varieties now in existence. Loss of any of them is a permanent loss to tropical agriculture and to the local people. Appropriate institutions should be established to maintain planting stocks of all of these, as well as of any other economic or potentially economic plants, for the future benefit of the islands.

4. *Fisheries*

Fisheries are basic in the native economy. Should marine resources become depleted, as they have during the war on certain islands, the people suffer. Therefore, along with efforts to develop fisheries, studies should be made to work out practical measures to maintain and increase these resources.

Subsistence fishing by native populations, using their traditional methods, rarely endangers the future supply. But for those species which enter into commerce, protective measures are essential. This is especially true of fish and shellfish inhabiting reefs and lagoons, because they can be taken so easily throughout the year; it applies also to such slow-growing animals as the sea turtles which come ashore to lay their eggs. The absolute necessity for preventing unrestricted capture of commercial species was recognized by the Japanese (who practiced conservation less from altruistic motives than for the fact that the marine products were valuable to homeland economy). The measures promulgated by the Japanese were based on scientific study, and the United States should push similar investigations. But, until new research demonstrates need for revisions, administration policy should be to reinstate the Japanese regulations, which are already familiar to the natives, and to extend scientific inquiry toward a better understanding of the marine biological problems involved.

5. *Historic Monuments*

Micronesia contains many historic monuments which will undoubtedly attract scientists and travelers to the islands and consequently add to native income. Archaeologic ruins at Ponape (Metalanim), Kusaie (Lele), and Tinian are among the many sites which should be preserved for posterity, including future generations of Micronesians.

6. *Conservation Commission*

Conservation is so important for the long-range future of Micronesia that the Board recommends the setting up of a conservation commission for Micronesia, with representation in each administrative field unit. Experience has shown that conservation cannot be left to casual sponsorship of officials apt to be preoccupied with more immediate problems.

A first and continuing job for the conservation commission will be an intensive investigation of fields requiring conservation programs, and the establishment of such programs. In this connection, study should be made of measures introduced during the Japanese regime. Also, it is known that native populations have evolved concepts and practices concerning many fields of conservation; these should be investigated with a view to adapting the useful ones to a program of conservation education. As a matter of fact, half the battle will be won if the Administration succeeds in implanting the general conservation idea in all natives' minds - through school programs, through training of native leaders, and through precept. Very important will be the example set by the American establishments in the islands. If the bulldozer continues to be the solution to all problems, it is expecting a lot to think that the natives are going to take seriously any conservation program advocated by Americans.[1]

G. EDUCATION FOR ECONOMIC DEVELOPMENT

Micronesians will, for better or worse, continue and expand their participation in western systems. In the kind of world we live in now, that is inevitable, and no one but a nostalgic antiquary would imagine otherwise. Luckily for Micronesians, contact with rather overwhelming institutions and gadgets will be softened: they will not have to fight for survival in competition with masses of colonists as they did during Japanese times and as other native peoples are having to do elsewhere in the Pacific; nor are their islands wealthy enough to attract commercial adventurers and fortune hunters. Actually, most of their contacts will be economic ones, and if programs similar to the kind advocated in this report finally materialize, Micronesians will not be unduly handicapped in these contacts.

These circumstances will provide the Administration with a unique and challenging opportunity, with a clear field, to introduce Micronesians to western systems by means of enlightened educational techniques. While a report on economy is not a proper context for a dissertation on the theory of native education, members of the Editorial Board do wish to record their belief that consideration of education in general and of vocational training in particular is relevant to economic planning. In the past many Micronesians learned Japanese ways by contact with Japanese colonists and in Japanese schools. They will now seek to learn more about western ways, the better to integrate their economy with that of the western world.

The authors of this Summary do not feel competent to handle adequately the large subject of vocational training, but would nevertheless like to propose certain principles:

1. English will eventually replace Japanese as the commercial contact language. To this end, professional linguists and educators should proceed at once with the task of systematizing orthographies of the various native languages and of compiling textbooks for the teaching of English. Modern methods of language instruction, which proved so proficient im military courses, should be adapted to Micronesian conditions, with emphasis on the teaching of words and concepts useful for economic relations.

2. School courses should be suited to the practical needs of natives; in most cases students will not care, or need, decade-long education in the niceties of western humanities.

3. Emphasis should be placed on preparing native teachers to train other natives, rather than on maintaining armies of American teachers, extension agents, home-demonstration agents, and so forth, in the field. A few carefully selected natives, thoroughly educated at instruction centers near to and comparable in environment to their home islands, will provide the native population with training better suited to local needs than could a host of peripatetic outsiders.

   Exceptionally well-qualified natives might be encouraged to continue their schooling in Hawaii or on the mainland, with the hope that they will return to their home islands and assume leadership as teachers.

4. Because of an urgent need for training along agricultural lines, the expedient should be adopted immediately of bringing a few mature and qualified native leaders to training centers for intensive four- to six-months' courses in agriculture. Instruction should embrace some of the elementary practices of horticulture, such as planting, budding and rooting of woody plants, selection of garden and planting sites, comparative advantages of vegetable and root crops, and diversification; recognition of insect pests and diseases, including an explanation of how they act and measures for control; soil and water character and relationships; poultry, hog, and cattle production and management, feeding and care. The purpose is to give natives an understanding of the biological and management processes with which they are concerned but not familiar, with the aim of increasing, diversifying, and perpetuating economic plants and animals.

5. Technical crafts instruction should be built around the needs of natives in carpentry for housebuilding and finished work, such as furniture; use and care of

tools; blacksmithing for fashioning tools, knives, iron work for boats, fishing equipment; cement work and construction practices, as for cisterns, steps, bollards, and rat proofing. Boatbuilding is a trade the natives know well, but they may gain in efficiency through carpentry and other crafts. The list of crafts could be extended.

Household arts, apart from nursing, could include handicraft manufacture, sewing, household and village sanitation, control of flies and rodents, preservation and cleanliness of water supply, disposal of wastes, and so forth.

Mechanical instruction in the elements and practice of navigation, piloting, and power-boat management should be undertaken among selected natives. Radio communication between the islands and headquarters stations could well be in the hands of native technicians, reporting meteorological data, emergency matters, ship arrivals, and news.[1]

H. ADMINISTRATION[1]

In general, the guiding principles thus far developed by Naval Military Government for the administration of economic affairs in Micronesia are sound. The two chief shortcomings are the lack of an integrated postwar plan at the policy-making level and the lack of implementation of the existing plans at the field level.

It is fully recognized that little could be done to overcome these handicaps during the past year owing to the demobilization of military personnel, the disruption of transportation facilities, the world-wide shortages in supplies, and the uncertainty over the future status of the islands. Some of these factors may continue to hamper planning and operations in the immediate period ahead. Nevertheless, it is vital to the success of the whole enterprise that the two shortcomings listed above be surmounted as swiftly as possible. The reasons for urging early decision and action are these: first, a master plan would end the threat of demoralization and disillusionment among the native population which may occur if present conditions persist much longer. Until the natives know with some degree of certitude what will occur, they are unable to make any permanent arrangements. Thus, they cannot rebuild their homes and cultivate the land until they know where their communities will be located. They see no point in trying to reconstruct their economy until they know the kind of life they will be able to have in the future. The natives are restless and are becoming increasingly anxious about their future. They have been assured many times that a major program would be forthcoming, and they now wonder if the United States will fulfill its obligations as a responsible government. Some native groups wonder if the government really intends to help them restore their prewar levels of living or whether it will abandon them to shift for themselves. They feel that they do not understand what America wishes to do in the islands. The natives have heard many speeches but no word of a long-range program. Each succeeding set of officers in the islands outlines a policy, the plans made under the preceding set are forgotten, and the natives are somewhat confused about America's full intentions. The improvisations of the war years were accepted as inevitable, but the war is now over, they point out, and little aid has been forthcoming to help them restore their livelihood, their homes, their communities, their way of life. All human beings require some goals to work toward; the absence of any long-range plan means the natives cannot formulate objectives to strive for. The formulation of a definite plan, even though its complete achievement must be postponed and its details modified, will evoke among the natives enthusiastic efforts, release energies now awaiting direction, and eliminate the tensions which now prevail.

Second, the declaration of our goals would enable the Administration to make permanent arrangements with native groups. It would provide perspective for the evaluation of needed actions and make for economy in the expenditure of efforts and funds. The officers in the field are unable to develop a comprehensive reconstruction program for the areas under their control. Officers are troubled by their inability to answer native inquiries about what they can count on and are forced to avoid commitments required before a going economy can be reëstablished. The recent requests for estimates of future budgetary requirements of each island elicited the feeling among the field personnel that they did not know what to report. There was no framework within which specifications could be decided upon. Also, there are no criteria for determining the types of supplies to order, for the kind of equipment to be requisitioned would depend on the ultimate objectives. A balanced economy is not being built and the divergencies between policies make for uncoördinated actions. Wages and prices are unrelated, government work projects absorb laborers essential for the reconstruction of subsistence facilities, workers are living away from homes when they are urgently needed in their villages to care for their dependents, and although Military Government and native governments are now united in a common effort to reach a common goal, each new problem is handled as a distinct entity on an emergency basis.

Hence it is urged that, if the long-range plans outlined in this report are deemed acceptable, they be acted upon as quickly as possible and outlined in full to the operating agencies and the natives. Should they be regarded as inadequate, then an alternative set of plans should be drafted and embarked upon at the earliest opportunity. Aggressive leadership by the Administration in the launching of any feasible plan will accrue to the benefit of both the United States and the Micronesians.

The implementation of present policies can be accomplished partially through strengthening the existing organization. Toward that end, the following specific courses of action are recommended. There is an immediate need for a clarification of the lines of authority between the present operating agencies, and ultimately for the unification of responsibility. The present division of functions is clearer at the high policy level than it is at the field level. It would assist materially to work out in detail the exact duties and relationships of the United States Commercial Company field agents and Military Government officers in respect to specific tasks. There is little uniformity in practice at present between islands. There is duplication of efforts in some spheres and gaps of activities in others because of the absence of a working division of labor. For the present, a careful delineation of specific activities would facilitate administration. From a long-range point of view, it would be desirable to develop a unified administrative staff. This could be done by transferring the civilian specialists to Administration payrolls and assigning to them assimilated rank. This has been successfully worked out by the occupation forces in Japan and Germany. Also, experts from other governmental agencies could be detailed to perform specialized duties for the Administration. This would preserve unity in administration and still provide for a diversity of technical services.

Much would be gained by the creation of a special corps with permanent duty assignments to this activity. It would be a major step toward providing the continuity which is now missing and yet which is so essential for responsible administration. By staggering the duty details, the personnel could overlap their periods of duty sufficiently to insure continuity within each unit and area. By making island administration a career, the type of personnel desired might be attracted and retained. Officials could acquire over the years the necessary experience for the competent performance of their functions. Reputation for outstanding ability could be earned, and the recognition thereof would give an incentive to officials. This would replace the present situation in which officers feel that their Military Government assignments are only temporary interludes and, thus, are impelled to leave this activity in order to advance their professional careers.

The addition of three technical sections, under a single division head at the present ComMarianas level, would enhance the effectiveness of the present organization. The three proposed sections are: statistics and reports; community analysis; interpreters.

The statistics and reports section would be charged with the development of standardized recording systems, the supervision of the collection of needed data, the summation of the factual information, and their presentation in a useful form to those requiring such data for policy and program decisions. There is not available a reportorial service providing adequate facts concerning current economic conditions to guide the administrator. The existing fragmentary records were compiled more by rough estimates than by actual enumeration. This section also should collaborate with the Bureau of the Census in the establishment of a decennial census. Guam has been included in the past in the United States census. It is recommended that all of the islands be covered in succeeding ones.

The community analysis section would be responsible for research into native affairs and problems confronting the Administration. It could be modeled after that which successfully operated in the War Relocation Authority in the United States and after the work of government anthropologists in the colonial administrations of Africa and the South Pacific. The administrator in the field does not have time nor is he in a position to make such surveys. Moreover, the training of the present administrative officers has prepared them to *use* cultural data in governing natives, but it has not trained them in the professional skills of *obtaining* such data by anthropological research. The findings of the economists and anthropologists of this Survey indicate the kinds of useful materials which can be collected. Members of the community analysis section could assist in the interpretation of native customs, help work out programs which take into account local institutions, ascertain the attitudes of the natives to various proposals, and appraise the practical effectiveness of measures under way. They would give the administrator the kinds of information he requires for realistic action. Experience elsewhere has demonstrated amply that the whole process of administration can be greatly eased by the use of such a staff.

The interpreters section would offer to field staffs, where required, language specialists to facilitate the process of communication. One of the major barriers to effective American-native coöperation at present is the difficulty of each understanding the other. It is not possible, as is now attempted in some areas, to rely on pidgin English and gestures for an adequate exchange of views. Efforts to do so give rise to misinterpretations which prevent the attainment of ends everyone wishes. There is little likelihood that the officers will master the native languages or that the natives will gain any degree of facility in English in the immediate periods ahead. Both would be desirable and should be encouraged, but neither can be counted upon for the present. The practice of using as an interpreter any native who can speak a bit of English should give way to a more satisfactory system. In numerous cases the interpreter has a marginal status in his own community and is exploiting his position for the benefit of a small group rather than using his talents for the welfare of all. This has become an especially acute problem in those places where a member of a minority group has been the chief intermediary between the population and the Administration. It is recommended that the use of Chamorros as interpreters outside of the Marianas be abandoned. A group of natives from all sections of the population should be selected for intensive training in the use of English and hired as interpreters. Even this will take a period of time. For the present it is recommended that Japanese-speaking interpreters be employed except where natives have a facility in English, as in Kusaie and the Marshalls. While it is undesirable to perpetuate this language, it is the only foreign language which most of the natives know. This would not solve the problem of communication with the older native generations who did not learn Japanese, but it would provide a more universal medium than now exists. There are numerous Americans of Japanese ancestry whose loyalty was demonstrated in the war and who would be willing to accept such work. Such Nisei should be trained in the cultural background of the area before being sent out to the field.

The total staff of these three sections would not be large. Yet they would perform extremely valuable functions which would substantially assist the operating agencies in fulfilling their missions with greater economy of effort and effectiveness than is now possible. This division could be attached to ComMarianas and serve the entire area in accordance with the need.

Four commissions to operate throughout the islands are needed: one to deal with land questions, one with wages, one for conservation, and another to handle the matter of claims.

The Claims Commission on Guam was authorized and established by statute to prove up and satisfy war claims of our nationals. Similar needs exist among natives in each of the other islands. Claims commissions should be established by the Administration and directed to accept cognizance of all claims by natives in other areas. Directives which have been issued to this effect should be implemented. Such commissions should be organized as aggressive fact-finding boards and directed to survey all of the islands to gather the necessary information, to hold hearings open to all natives in each area, and to make specific recommendations. This would not be as difficult an assignment as might appear: in every native community there are individuals qualified to do most of the fact finding and recording. The commission should be headed by an administrative official and contain both American and native representatives to pass on claims. Appeals from the decision of the commission should be permitted through the judiciary system outlined below.

A land office of the type proposed in the section on Land (see Chapter II, section A) should be organized. As proposed for the claims commission, attention should be directed immediately to the settlement of land questions and to the codification of land laws. Its personnel should include an Administration official as its head and be composed of both administrative and native members. Provisions for appeal should be made either through the courts or through a series of higher boards. If the latter is preferred, two successive levels should be provided. The intermediary level would review the evidence and be authorized to make on-the-spot investigations if necessary. Its membership should include both administrative and native personnel. The highest review board should be appointed by a Cabinet-level official and have final authority over land questions.

A program should be formulated for the greater exchange of views between native leadership and the heads of the Administration. It is recommended that at regular intervals the native chiefs and other delegated representatives be invited to Guam to discuss economic and related matters with Administration staffs. These delegates would not constitute an administrative body but would merely provide an opportunity for the informal discussion of common problems. This would provide, also, a chance for the responsible leaders of natives from the various islands to work out trade relations among themselves.

Attention is called to the need for continued follow-through on the directive recently issued by CinCPac-CinCPOA which concerns the relationship of shore establishments to Military Government. The tendency in some areas has been to regard the administration of native affairs as serving the shore bases rather than as an essential function in its own right. This perspective was necessary during the war, but now it seriously hampers the reconstruction of the native economy. The relationship between these two units should be further clarified by specific directives on supply, labor, land use, personnel, and similar subjects. Without such guidance from the higher echelons, the field staffs in Military Government are unduly restricted in their efforts.

The principles of self-government already have been endorsed by the Administration. These principles are also applicable to economic affairs. If self-dependency is to be fostered, it will require diligent and patient efforts on the part of the field personnel. Native societies do not make crucial decisions without prolonged discussion among the members of the group. No chief is free to command his people without lengthy consultations and their prior approval. The tendency has been to present an issue to the native representatives and ask for an immediate decision. Representatives of native groups should be given ample opportunity to consider a matter before being called upon for final decision. Much can be accomplished positively if natives are led rather than pushed into channels which are intended for their economic benefit. Micronesians have had much experience with previous administrations in which they have learned how to offset decisions imposed from the outside. Tales told by them in a half boastful manner about circumventing or thwarting Japanese administrators with whom they did not agree are pertinent evidence. Relationships within a military organization must be based on discipline in which orders are issued and carried out. But the same orientation cannot be used by officers in dealing with natives in the designated spheres of self-government. To do so will reduce self-government to a mere ritual, as has occurred on some islands. So, too, attempts to bring about economic reform in conformance with western modes of living, before the natives are ready to make the changes, would undermine their faith in our avowed intentions. Natives should be given the opportunity of learning about and considering cultural alternatives, but the desire for change should come from within the society. No penalties in any form should be invoked for refusal to accept a proposed change over which they were told they had a free choice. Natives should be encouraged and assisted to assume responsibility for and operation of self-government. They have in the past conducted their own affairs with reasonable satisfaction. A large measure of responsibility for satisfactory operation of local government now resides in native custom, local native officials, and local governing groups. The policy of American government and of local governing officials should be to encourage continuation and extension of local responsibilities not only for political matters but also for promotion of appropriate economic enterprises. Government controls should be exercised to assist natives to become self-dependent and not to restrict their actions merely to control them. This is one of the most challenging issues which confronts the Administration in Micronesia today.

To achieve the above goal natives should be informed, after appropriate counsel and agreement with them, concerning the spheres and ranges in which they retain full responsibility, and concerning those in which responsibility is to be shared with officials representing the outside authority. American governing officials should draw up and present, pursuant to appropriate clearance, a statement of the principles, rules, regulations, and administrative policies which apply to government of natives in specific areas. This should state the rights of the governing officials and the rights of the natives. This statement should include, for example, very explicit sections concerning ownership and responsibility of resources and property lent or given to native communities by the Administration.

A new judicial system should be established. Native laws require codification and formal sanctioning after review by proper authority. Only where local laws conflict with the principles of American law or military security should they be overruled.[2] Special efforts should be directed to the selection of reputable and responsible natives who may assume judicial roles in the settlement of native conflicts and in the trying of cases arising within native governmental spheres of responsibility. Special efforts also should be directed toward achieving the adoption of native judicial functions in trying cases which arise in the field of joint responsibility in order better to promote wise and prudent dispensation of justice as well as to relieve governing officials of administrative burdens. An appeals procedure should be formulated whereby natives may appeal their cases to a higher regional court at Guam and finally into the Federal courts. Legislation will be required to authorize this legal procedure, but the technical problems involved are not major. Natives should have the same legal rights in the courts of the United States as citizens have.

To assist the Islands Administration in the formulation of practical means for achieving desired ends, it is suggested that a technical advisory board be created in Washington. This board of technical experts should not deal with policy questions but rather develop practical methods for handling specific technical problems. It would work on such subjects as plant quarantine, protection of marine resources, nutrition, child care, textbooks, and school curriculum. This would entail establishing liaison with Federal departments and agencies working in these fields rather than duplicating their work. The Bureaus of Animal Industry and Plant Industry in the Department of Agriculture, Fisheries and Wildlife in the Department of the Interior, the Bureau of Education, and so forth, illustrate the types of skills which could be drawn upon.

Before this section is closed, attention should again be directed to the fact that islands throughout Micronesia differ greatly with respect to the kinds of administrative services they require. Places such as Ulithi, Sonsorol, and Kapingamarangi, with small populations, simple economics, and isolation from main centers, will not be as closely supervised or as extensively aided as will places such as Guam, Saipan, and Palau. It may not be necessary to place administrative personnel permanently on the small outpost islands, but special provisions should be made to insure that they are not neglected. (Consideration might well be given to requiring that certain officials devote all their time in the interests of the outposts.) Outposts should be visited regularly, although not necessarily frequently, and their populations should be specially assisted to become more self-sufficient because of their greater isolation.

The wartime task of administration has been completed. The programs essential for the governing of the natives during the war do not meet the needs of administrators or administered in the postwar period. The natives look to American leadership. Only through that leadership can the islands be restored to their prewar level. The investment of funds and efforts to attain the ends outlined in this report at this crucial time will pay dividends in economy of expenditure over the years and in native loyalty and will offer evidence of American moral leadership in relationship to dependent peoples. From a purely practical standpoint, it will make possible an economic system in the islands which will enable the natives to become self-sustaining once more and be an asset rather than a liability to the United States.

Notes

B. FINANCE

1. This and following paragraphs require some revision in view of changes made since 1946. The United States Commercial Company has been succeeded by the Island Trading Company. Native traders are now encouraged and assisted in making direct transactions with mainland firms. And new price directives have insured that native producers and consumers will receive pricing benefits just short of general subsidy.

2. By 1949 some progress had been made in the kind of financing envisaged here. The Bank of Guam and its Saipan branch make loans to municipalities and groups and individuals for financing various kinds of enterprises; and in the other islands Naval Government officials are authorized to do likewise.

3. The Saipan branch of the Bank of Guam had, by 1949, become an established institution; and elsewhere throughout the Territory Naval Government units were authorized to serve as savings depositories. Some natives from outlying islands were, in fact, being sent to Guam for training in banking procedures, in order to extend the bank's regular services throughout the Territory.

4. See footnote 2, above.

5. Since 1946 the Naval Government has installed a tax and appropriations system which does, in fact, follow quite closely the recommendations recorded by the Survey economists.

C. PUBLIC FACILITIES

1. Since 1946 the Administration has also assisted with the rebuilding of men's clubhouses in such places as Palau and Yap, where these structures constituted such important centers for group activity.

2. In addition, by 1949 natives in one district of Ponape were already operating a hydroelectric power station of their own.

D. TRANSPORTATION

1. By 1949 interisland transport throughout the Territory had been established on a fairly frequent and reliable basis, so that many of the statements made in this section require revision.

2. By 1949 a bus service had been installed on Saipan.

E. COMMUNICATION

1. See note 1 to section D.

F. CONSERVATION

1. These recommendations have been vigorously followed up by the Naval Administration in coöperation with the Pacific Science Board of the National Research Council, with the result that, by 1949, a conservation officer had been added to the Administration staff of the Territory, with assurances of firm support for initiating programs such as those advocated here. See "Conservation in Micronesia," compiled by Harold J. Coolidge (Washington, D.C.: National Research Council, 1948).

G. EDUCATION FOR ECONOMIC DEVELOPMENT

1. In 1948 the Administration appointed an Advisory Committee on Education for Guam and the Trust Territory and sent this group of experts to the islands, where they observed at first hand the educational needs and resources of the islanders and prepared a series of recommendations which endorse to a gratifying degree those made here. Also, expert linguists have been sent to the field to systematize native orthographies; facilities have been created for elementary and advanced agricultural and vocational training; and an agricultural extension officer has been detailed to the administrative staff.

H. ADMINISTRATION

1. Far-reaching administrative changes have taken place since this chapter was written. For example, the former Japanese islands now constitute a strategic Trust Territory, and administration of native peoples has become more civilian - in form, at least. The United States Commercial Company has been succeeded by the Island Trading Company, which comes directly under Naval Government and hence does not require the sort of "coördination" with naval activities recommended by the 1946 Survey team. To describe adequately all the administrative changes which have taken place since 1946 would require another chapter equally long; hence, the reader interested in learning about the current situation is advised to read "An Outline of the Activities in the Trust Territory of the Pacific Islands under Naval Administration to 1 October 1948," obtainable in the Navy Department, Washington, D.C. Of major importance for administration was the CIMA (Coördinated Investigation of Micronesian Anthropology) project sponsored by the Pacific Science Board of the National Research Council and financed by the Navy and the Viking Fund. Under these auspices, social scientists from several universities and foundations were sent to Micronesia to study native institutions.

2. This recommendation obviously requires qualification; the original implication concerned such "local laws" or conventions as infanticide, usurious practices, and so forth.

CHAPTER V. CONCLUSION

Why should the United States government support an extensive and costly program such as that recommended in this Summary?

Our government has assumed the obligation to promote economic development of Micronesia. Is it not the least we can do to restore the economy to the prewar level? Even though this will prove costly in the beginning, it is our government's responsibility and the logical consequence of our commitments. We have excised most of Micronesia from its former position in the Japanese Empire, from an economic setting in which real income of the native was far higher than it is now likely to be without assistance of all kinds.

Who is responsible for this situation?

Japan? Certainly, to some extent, as one facet of her war guilt. But from a practical point of view, how can she be made to underwrite Micronesia's economic recovery?

The United States? Certainly not, in the sense that she precipitated the series of events leading up to the situations; but the United States has inherited the problem and *does not seem eager to turn it over to some other power to solve.*

The Micronesians? In no possible sense can they be considered responsible for their present predicament; nor does it appear that they will be permitted the absolute freedom of choice to decide their own destinies.

It is compelling, therefore, that, as long as the United States government restricts Micronesians' freedom of complete choice in any way and does not choose to share the assets of Micronesia along with its liabilities, it cannot escape the full consequences of guaranteeing Micronesians their economic well being. Its obligation to them is even greater than it is to its own citizens, who – in the final analysis – enjoy much greater freedom of action.

Bei Fragen zur Produktsicherheit wenden Sie sich bitte an:
If you have any questions regarding product safety,
please contact:

Walter de Gruyter GmbH
Genthiner Straße 13
10785 Berlin
productsafety@degruyterbrill.com